IN GOD WE TRUST

How the

Supreme Court's

First Amendment decisions

affect

organized religion.

IN GOD WE TRUST

KATHRYN PAGE CAMP

Foreword by John W. Mauck

FaithWalk
PUBLISHING

Grand Haven, Michigan

Published by FaithWalk Publishing
Grand Haven, Michigan 49417

Printed in the United States of America
11 10 09 08 07 06   7 6 5 4 3 2 1

Library of Congress Cataloging-in-Publication Data

Camp, Kathryn Page.
 In God we trust : how the Supreme Court's First Amendment decisions affect organized religion / by Kathryn Page Camp.
    p. cm.
 ISBN-13: 978-1-932902-60-0 (pbk. : alk. paper)
 ISBN-10: 1-932902-60-0 (pbk. : alk. paper)
 1. Church and state—United States. 2. United States—Church history. 3. United States—Religion. 4. Christianity and law. 5. United States. Constitution. 1st Amendment. I. Title.
 BR516.C28 2006
 342.7308'52–dc22
                    2006009127

DEDICATION

This book is dedicated to the God I trust and to Roland, Caroline, and John for the joy they bring into my life.

CONTENTS

FOREWORD

Secular legions and religious activists are contending as never before over the soul of America. On the legal front of this wide-ranging Culture War, each side claims to argue from the constitutional/historical high ground. Amidst the confusion these conflicting claims create, we who care about that "soul," our souls, and those of our families and communities, are often at a loss in separating truth from spin.

To the rescue: Kathryn Page Camp. To the prelaw student, pastor, reporter, high school teacher, generalist lawyer or judge, voter, and every culture-war concerned American, Ms. Camp has thrown a lifeline. *In God We Trust* transforms the daunting complexity of free exercise jurisprudence into a clear, simple and enjoyable primer on when and how the American legal system resolves religious disputes.

Starting with the founding fathers, she recounts historical controversies that gave birth to the Constitution, the Bill of Rights, and particularly the First Amendment. The narrative is enlivened by insightful and sometimes amusing anecdotes concerning Jefferson, Madison, and other giants (and pygmies) whose personalities and concerns still vitally affect our lives today.

Once the framework for the development of law through the Supreme Court is explained, Ms. Camp takes the reader on a case-thumbnail stroll of their decisions. Because she always includes interesting details concerning the people in the legal battles, the stories and legal principles that emerge register. The cases are arranged through a comfortable blend of chronology and topic so that the Supreme Court's approach to areas of religious litigation such as church property disputes, individual conscience issues, and freedom to speak about faith are understood as they develop both from precedents in the same area and from the broader legal and social trends shaping the law at various points in history. Throughout, Ms. Camp identifies instances where the underlying logic of a Supreme Court decision is not well explained or is difficult to square with prior or subsequent rulings. In those situations, exhibiting a humility uncharacteristic for a knowledgeable lawyer, she never imposes a solution but rather allows the reader to reach his or her own conclusions or simply adjust to the reality that the "certainty" that law projects to society is actually considerably more ambiguous than some of the Culture War generals would have us believe.

Thoughtful readers will avoid the impulse to download *In God We Trust* into their mental databanks and pause to reflect on questions raised by the author. Thus, the Holy Spirit will have the opportunity to integrate into their hearts the important information presented, thereby producing his desired effect: Trust in God.

—John Mauck

John Mauck is a Chicago attorney whose practice concentrates on religious freedom litigation; he is the author of *Paul on Trial: The Book of Acts as a Defense of Christianity.*

ACKNOWLEDGMENTS

I cannot possibly thank everyone who helped, supported, and encouraged me as I wrote this book, but a few deserve special mention. Thanks to Dan Roth for his encouragement and support. Thanks to the Highland Writer's Group, led by Larry and Sharon Ginensky, for critiquing the manuscript and Carole King for help in editing it. I also thank my publisher, Dirk Wierenga; my editor, Louann Werksma; and Dirk's assistant, Ginny McFadden. Last but not least, I appreciate the loving support of my husband, Roland, and my children, Caroline and John.

INTRODUCTION

*I*t was 1962, and the biggest religious controversy my small town had struggled with was whether the Roman Catholic priest or the Presbyterian minister would officiate at the public high school's baccalaureate service. But a much bigger religious controversy was brewing in Washington, D.C. The Supreme Court had been asked to decide if the First Amendment to the United States Constitution prohibited state-sponsored prayers in public schools.

The storm created by that controversy still rages. The Supreme Court's 1962 decision in *Engel v. Vitale* answered the immediate question (yes, the First Amendment prohibits state-sponsored prayer) but raised others. What did our forefathers mean by the words they used in the religion clauses of the First Amendment? And has the Supreme Court been true to that original intent?

I do not presume to know the answers to those questions. Although I have my own opinions, they are just that—opinions, not facts. So I am not going to impose them on you. Instead, I wrote this book to provide you with the information you need to reach your own conclusions.

The information I have included is, by necessity, selective. If I were to cover every bit of historical information that scholars have used to argue the meaning of the religion clauses, this would be a multi-volume set. And if it included the District and Circuit Court cases, as well as the Supreme Court cases, it would fill a shelf. Instead, I have attempted to select the most relevant information, regardless of its point of view, and to use it in context.

I do not, however, guarantee that this book is 100% neutral. Although I have attempted to be objective in selecting and summarizing the material, even a "neutral" evaluation is inevitably colored by the evaluator's own opinions. But I have done the best I can.

You may get more out of this book if you try to answer the questions at the end of each chapter. There are no right or wrong answers, but the questions will help you think about what you have just read. And the whole purpose of this book is to help you reach your own conclusions.

I hope you have an enjoyable learning experience.

CHAPTER ONE
THE QUESTION

Cane County has had a gang problem for many years, and the high school dress code bans clothing and jewelry with gang symbols. But one gang is now wearing a particular type of cross to identify its members. When confronted by school authorities, the gang members claim the cross is a religious symbol. Not knowing what else to do, the Cane County School Board revises the dress code to ban clothing and jewelry with religious as well as gang symbols.

Cindy and Ben are students at Cane County High School. Cindy wears a cross necklace to show her Christian faith, and Ben wears a Star of David lapel pin as a symbol of his Jewish faith. Unfortunately, they can no longer wear their religious jewelry during the school day without violating the dress code.

So what rights do Cindy and Ben have? Does the school board's action violate the Establishment Clause, the Free Exercise Clause, or the Free Speech Clause of the First Amendment? The answer to that question lies in the hands of nine people—the Justices who serve on the United States Supreme Court.

United States citizens do not have to look very far to find reminders of their country's religious heritage. Every piece of money (coin or bill) says "In God We Trust"; Congress opens each daily session with prayer; and even the Supreme Court chambers contain pictures of the Ten Commandments.[1] Some reminders are as old as the country itself, while others are more recent; although the Pledge of Allegiance was written in 1892, the words "under God" were not added until 1954.

But the signs of America's diversity are almost as prominent. A plaque inside the base of the Statue of Liberty invites all countries and all religions to "give me ... your huddled masses yearning to breathe free." Most of America's big cities have a China Town, a German Town, and Arabic, Jewish, and Irish neighborhoods. Even the small Midwestern city of Madison, Wisconsin—population 200,000—is home to members of the Baha'i, Islam, Buddhist, Mormon, and Jewish religions as well as members of Catholic, Eastern Orthodox, and Protestant churches.[2]

Against this background, what do Americans mean when they say they have religious freedom? Or, more specifically, what does the First Amendment mean when it says, "Congress shall make no law respecting an establishment of religion, or prohibiting the free exercise thereof; or abridging the freedom of speech"? That is the question.

... the founding fathers created a system of checks and balances that gives the judicial branch the final say. And imperfect though the system may be, most citizens of the United States are unwilling to trade it for any of the systems existing in other countries. That means the Supreme Court is stuck with the job, and America must live with its answers.

So what is the debate about? For some, it is a fight for religious freedom. For others, it is a fight against religious tyranny. And for both, it is a debate over the original meaning of the First Amendment's religion clauses.

It is the Supreme Court's job to judge the debate and answer the question. Unfortunately, even the Justices cannot agree on the answer, and the language in the First Amendment does not provide it. Just what is a law "respecting an establishment of religion"? It would be simple if the clause stated that Congress could not "establish a church" or "prefer one religion over another" or "provide aid to any religious organization." But the founding fathers did not make it that easy.

So how does the Supreme Court decide what the Establishment Clause means? It follows specific rules that create a hierarchy. At the top of the hierarchy is the language itself. If the language does not answer the question, then the Court looks to the direct legislative history—the contemporaneous words and actions of the lawmakers who voted on the clause.

Finally, the indirect legislative history—actions and events that preceded the clause or that occurred outside of the legislative chambers while the clause was being debated and adopted—is at the bottom of the hierarchy. These rules will be discussed in the next chapter.

Does the Court always get the answer right? Of course not. Supreme Court Justices are human. But someone has to decide, and the founding fathers created a system of checks and balances that gives the judicial branch the final say. And imperfect though the system may be, most citizens of the United States are unwilling to trade it for any of the systems existing in other countries. That means the Supreme Court is stuck with the job, and America must live with its answers.

The First Amendment contains three clauses that figure in many Supreme Court cases involving religion and religious activities. They are:

- the Establishment Clause ("Congress shall make no law respecting an establishment of religion")
- the Free Exercise Clause ("or prohibiting the free exercise thereof")
- the Free Speech Clause ("or abridging the freedom of speech")

The language in these clauses is very general, which makes it difficult for the courts to interpret and apply them. But it also gives the Constitution room to grow as circumstances change. So how does the First Amendment apply to real-life situations that the founders may not have foreseen? The hypothetical case introduced at the beginning of this chapter is just one unanticipated situation. The following hypothetical cases illustrate some others.

A Town with Heart

Milton Jones, a lifetime resident of the small town of Heart, leaves some money to the town when he dies. His will directs that the town use the money to erect a statue of Mother Theresa in the town square as a reminder that the town stands for "loving our neighbors, helping the poor, and having an open heart." Although the town board agrees to the terms of the bequest, a small group of citizens objects, claiming that placing a statute of a religious person in the town square would violate the Establishment Clause.

The Prison Bible Study

Michael, David, Isaiah, and Emilio are Adams Correctional Center inmates who have become Christians during their incarceration. They attend worship services at the prison every Sunday morning and a weekly Bible study, led by the prison chaplain, every Wednesday evening. They are hungry for more group Bible study, however, and would like to meet together daily during the evening recreation period. The prisoner's lounge is too noisy, so they request permission to meet in a cell, where they are willing to be locked in.

Prison officials do not allow prisoners to meet in small groups because they could conspire against prison officials, plan a prison break, or foster gang loyalty. Also, the prison guards do not patrol the cell block during recreation periods. So the administration denies the request as against prison policy. Michael, David, Isaiah, and Emilio claim that the denial violates their rights under the Free Exercise Clause.

A Christmas Cross

Bob and Karen Harris are frustrated with the commercialism of Christmas. They want to remind their neighbors that the season is all about Christ, so they put up a 4-foot-tall, lighted manger scene in their yard. The display complies with the suburb's residential zoning ordinance, which prohibits free-standing figures higher than four feet in residential neighborhoods. Unfortunately, no one notices Bob and Karen's display because they live between two houses that cram their yards full of Santas, reindeer, snowmen, and other secular symbols—all four feet or less.

The next year Bob and Karen decide to make their display more prominent by adding an 8-foot-tall wooden cross behind the manger scene. They outline the cross with strings of white lights and place a lighted star at the crossbeam. The Harrises do not have anything else in their yard except some icicle lights hanging from the eves, so their display is more sedate and tasteful than the neighbors' displays. Still, it violates the zoning ordinance, and the suburb fines Bob and Karen $100 for every day the cross remains up. They challenge the fine, claiming the zoning ordinance violates the Free Speech Clause as applied to their display.

These hypothetical cases may resemble actual lawsuits in the lower courts, but they are not drawn from any particular case; and, as of this writing, the Supreme Court has not considered their particular facts. They are included to show that the First Amendment affects real people in their everyday lives and to provide a framework for the discussion in later chapters.

This book endeavors to provide insight into how the Justices decide what the First Amendment means. It will also give readers the tools to answer the question for themselves–or to decide that the question is unanswerable. It will do so by explaining the main principles of interpretation, summarizing the amendment's legislative history, and describing the cases giving the Supreme Court's answers.

In the next chapter, we will begin with the rules that the Court follows.

Questions

At the end of each chapter in this book, there will be two questions. Answer each one and explain your responses. Then see if your answers change as you read this book.

Question 1: Rewrite the First Amendment in your own words to say what you believe it means.

Question 2: How do you think the Supreme Court would respond to the four hypothetical situations described in this chapter?

    a. Can the Cane County School Board ban clothing and jewelry with religious symbols?

    b. Can Heart put a statue of Mother Theresa in the town square?

    c. Must the prison allow Michael, David, Isaiah, and Emilio to hold a Bible study in a quiet area during their recreation period?

    d. Does the ordinance prohibiting the Harrises from putting up an 8-foot cross violate their right to free speech?

CHAPTER TWO
PLAYING BY THE RULES

She was too young to speak for herself, so her father decided to do it for her. He asked the courts to ban the Pledge of Allegiance from her kindergarten classroom unless the words "under God" were removed. But did Michael Newdow really speak for his daughter? Her mother did not think so, and the U.S. Supreme Court agreed.[1] So he could not use the courts to challenge the Pledge.

Why does it matter who files a lawsuit? And how does a case get to the Supreme Court anyway? The court system has its own rules, and both the parties and the judges must follow them.

Most cases involving the Constitution and the Bill of Rights may be filed in either state or federal court.[2] In both systems they start in a trial court, with a single judge hearing the case.[3]

In most states, the losing party can appeal the case to an intermediate state court, where it will usually be heard by a panel of three judges.[4] A few of the smaller or less populated states do not have intermediate courts, however.[5] In those states, cases are appealed from the lowest court directly to the highest one.

When a case is appealed to the state's highest court, that court may be required to hear the case or may have discretion to reject it, in which case the decision from the last court stands. Usually, a case filed in state court must go all the way through the state court system before the U.S. Supreme Court will hear it. Once the highest state court has either decided it or refused to hear it, however, it can go directly to the U.S. Supreme Court.

In the federal court system, federal district courts are the trial courts. The losing party can appeal a decision from a district court to the federal circuit court of appeals for the circuit where the district court is located.[6] The appeal to the circuit court is usually an appeal of right, meaning that the circuit court must hear it.

A panel of three judges hears the appeal. Because of the large number of cases that are appealed, each circuit draws from a pool of circuit judges, and the cases are assigned to give each circuit judge an equal case load. If the circuit's caseload is especially large, or if it has a number of judicial vacancies, the panel may include a district court judge sitting by designation.

A party that does not like the panel's decision can petition the circuit for a rehearing *en banc*. If judges grant the petition, all of the circuit court judges from that circuit hear the case. Petitions for rehearing *en banc* are rarely granted, however.

So how do cases get to the U.S. Supreme Court? Whether the case comes through the state or the federal courts, the losing party files a petition for *certiorari*—often referred to simply as "cert." A petition for certiorari is discretionary with the Supreme Court, and at least four justices must vote to grant it. The Court usually hears a case only if there is a split between the circuits (meaning that the appeals courts in two circuits have decided the same issue the opposite way) or the legal principle involved in the case is particularly important.

The U.S. Supreme Court is made up of nine justices appointed by the President and confirmed by the Senate. All of the justices hear every case if they are available and do not have conflicts or relationships with the parties. If there are vacancies on the Court, or if a justice cannot participate, the remaining justices hear the case.

Supreme Court cases are decided by majority vote. So what happens if the vote is tied? The last decision stands, and whoever won at the Circuit Court of Appeals (if the case came through the federal courts) or the highest state court wins the Supreme Court case.

Many Supreme Court cases have more than one written opinion. If a majority of the Justices agrees on the reasons for the decision, the opinion announcing those reasons is the opinion of the Court. Justices who agree with the result and some but not all of the reasoning or who want to further explain why they voted as they did can file concurring opinions. If they agree with the result but not the reasons, they can file opinions concurring in the result. If they disagree with the result, they can file dissenting opinions. The opinion of the Court is reported first, followed by concurring opinions. Dissenting opinions are reported last.

If a majority agrees on the result but not the reasoning, or if the vote is tied, there is no opinion of the Court. Instead, the Justice who represents the plurality reasoning will announce the result, and his or her opinion will be the first opinion reported. The reasoning in that decision does not control later decisions, however. Similarly, concurring and dissenting opinions provide insight into the Justices' thinking but do not carry the same weight as the opinion of the Court.

The first question the federal courts ask is whether they have to interpret the U.S. Constitution. Because the Constitution is the supreme law of the land and any interpretation is likely to have far-ranging effects, the courts will not rule on constitutional questions if they can avoid them.[7]

One way the courts avoid—or at least delay—constitutional issues is by requiring parties to exhaust their administrative remedies. In *Ohio Civil Rights Commission v. Dayton Christian Schools, Inc.* (1986), the school corporation told teacher Linda Hoskinson that it would not renew her employment contract for the next year. Linda was pregnant, and the Christian bodies that ran the schools believed that mothers should stay home with their young children.[8] After Linda threatened to sue for sex discrimination, the school rescinded its nonrenewal decision but fired her because she had not pursued her complaint through the biblical chain of command, as required by her employment contract. Linda then filed a complaint with the Ohio Civil Rights Commission.

After investigating the allegations, the Commission initiated an administrative proceeding against the school. The school answered the Commission's complaint by claiming that it acted on its sincerely held religious belief, so the First Amendment prohibited the Commission from hearing Linda's claim. The school corporation also filed a lawsuit in federal court seeking to prevent the Commission from continuing with its case.

When reviewing the federal action, the Supreme Court decided that the federal courts should have rejected the case because the school had not exhausted its administrative remedies. In other words, the courts should have allowed the Commission to decide the case first. After all, if it had ruled in favor of the school, there would be no reason for the federal courts to get involved.

Federal courts may also refuse to decide constitutional challenges to state and local laws if the state courts have not had a chance to interpret those laws. In a free exercise case, for example, maybe the state courts could interpret the law so that it does not prohibit the religious conduct at issue. If that is a possibility, the federal courts will not rule on the constitutionality of that law until after the highest state court has said what it means or how the court will apply it to the facts in the case. This was the U.S. Supreme Court's approach in the 1947 case of *Rescue Army v. Municipal Court of Los Angeles.*[9]

Rescue Army was a religious organization that solicited money and secondhand articles to aid people who were in need. Los Angeles passed an ordinance requiring everyone who solicited contributions in public areas "by means of a box or receptacle" to register with the city and post an information card at the collection site. The Rescue Army believed that the First Amendment's guarantee of religious freedom prohibited the city from applying the ordinance to its activities, so it continued to solicit money and donations without complying with the ordinance. The city arrested an officer of the Rescue Army for violating the ordinance, and the Rescue Army sued to enjoin the city from enforcing it.

Although the U.S. Supreme Court considered the Rescue Army's case, it did not reach the constitutional issue. Instead, it noted that the California Supreme Court said the ordinance was constitutional but left a lot of questions unanswered about how it would be applied. So it was unclear if the Rescue Army officer would be found guilty in his criminal trial. The U.S. Supreme Court then sent the case back to the state courts.

Similarly, if the federal courts can legitimately interpret a federal law to avoid constitutional issues, that is what they will do. In *NLRB v. Catholic Bishop of Chicago* (1979), the National Labor Relations Board certified teachers' unions for Catholic school teachers in Chicago, Illinois, and Fort Wayne, Indiana.[10] The two Catholic bodies challenged the NLRB's authority, claiming that the National Labor Relations Act did not authorize the NLRB to certify unions at schools run by religious groups and, if it did, that authority would violate their rights under the religion clauses of the First Amendment. The Court avoided the constitutional issue by reviewing the Act's legislative history and finding that Congress did not intend to give the NLRB authority over private religious schools.

Standing

Another basis for avoiding constitutional issues is standing—or, rather, the lack of standing. Standing is the right to bring a lawsuit. If anyone could sue about anything, the courts would be so backlogged that nothing would get heard. And if the person bringing the case does not have a concrete interest in the outcome, the result might be different from what it would be if it was brought by someone directly affected by the facts and able to point out all the practical questions they raise.

To avoid these problems, the law requires the plaintiff—the person who files the case—to meet three tests. First, the plaintiff must have suffered an "injury in fact," which must be concrete rather than theoretical. Second, the injury has to result from the activity that is the subject of the lawsuit. Third, the lawsuit must be able to right the wrong done to the plaintiff, or at least lessen it, if the plaintiff proves the wrong and the injury.[11] Two First Amendment cases illustrate the standing requirement.

Doremus v. Board of Education (1952)[12]
A New Jersey law provided for public schools to read five verses

of the Old Testament, without comment, at the beginning of each school day. Two taxpayers filed a lawsuit asking for a declaratory judgment that the law was unconstitutional under the Establishment Clause of the First Amendment. The Supreme Court held that the plaintiffs' status as taxpayers did not give them standing since the New Jersey law did not affect their taxes. One of the plaintiffs did have a daughter in a high school where the daily Bible readings occurred, but the complaint did not allege that the readings had harmed or even offended the daughter. So the plaintiffs had not shown that the law had injured them. Additionally, the daughter had graduated by the time the case reached the Supreme Court, so a decision that the New Jersey law was unconstitutional would not right the wrong to her, even if there were one. Therefore, the Supreme Court held that the plaintiffs did not have standing and could not challenge the constitutionality of the New Jersey law.

Elk Grove Unified School District v. Newdow (2004) [13]
In the case mentioned at the beginning of this chapter, Michael Newdow wanted to enjoin his daughter's school district from using the Pledge of Allegiance because it contained the words "under God." Rather than deciding whether the school's use of the Pledge violated the First Amendment, the Supreme Court said Newdow did not have standing to bring the case on his daughter's behalf. Her mother objected to the lawsuit on two grounds: because her daughter was a Christian who had no objection to saying the words in the Pledge, and because she was afraid her daughter might be harmed if people thought she shared Michael Newdow's atheist beliefs. Although the girl's parents had joint legal custody at the time the case reached the Supreme Court, the custody decree gave the mother the final say when the parents disagreed. Since they did not agree on the lawsuit, Newdow could not bring the case on his daughter's behalf. And he did not have a direct enough interest to bring it on his own behalf, so he simply could not bring it at all.

This principle—that the courts will not decide constitutional issues if they can decide the case on other grounds—does not mean that courts will never hear those issues. It just keeps them from getting heard prematurely when the questions they raise are merely theoretical. As will be discussed in Chapter 6, the U.S. Supreme Court decided the constitutional issue in *Doremus* ten years later.[14]

When it is finally time to decide a constitutional issue—or any other legal issue—the lower courts must follow the decisions of the courts above them. State trial courts must follow the decisions of that state's appeals courts (including its highest court), and the state appeals courts must follow the decisions of the state's highest court. Federal district courts must follow the decisions of the circuit court for the circuit they are located in, and all federal courts must follow the decisions of the U.S. Supreme Court. Federal judges follow state court decisions if they are interpreting that state's laws, and state judges follow federal court decisions if they are interpreting federal law. Higher courts do not have to follow decisions by lower courts, and federal district courts do not have to follow decisions from circuit courts other than their own, although they do consider them.

Previously decided cases that the courts recognize as authority are called *precedents.* Not every decision is a precedent, however. In some situations, the court deciding the case will limit it to its facts or declare that it is not important enough to be used as precedent. In other situations, a decision by a higher court will overrule a lower court case either expressly or by implication (where the higher court reaches the opposite conclusion in a similar but different case); and on rare occasions a court will even overrule one of its own earlier cases. None of these is a precedent.

If a case is a precedent, however, then lower courts are required to follow it if it applies, and the court that decided the precedential case should also follow it unless there are grounds to overrule or distinguish it. This principle is called "*stare decisis,*" and it is a doctrine created by the courts, not by the Constitution.[15]

The courts created the doctrine for a very simple reason: People need to know what the law is. Suppose Jack buys a hill from the previous owner, builds a house on it, and wants to go on vacation, but Jill wants the hill and the house and threatens to move in while he is away. If Jack knows that every judge will say "You paid for it, it's yours," then he can go on vacation without worrying. If he knows every judge will say, "Possession is nine-tenths of the law," then he will stay home. But if one judge could say "You paid for it, it's yours," and another judge could say "Possession is nine-tenths of the law," how does he make plans? To paraphrase Justice Brandeis, most of the time it is more important for the law to be known than it is for the law to be right.[16]

Because the courts created *stare decisis,* however, they can also decide not to apply it if they believe the law is better served by overruling a previous precedent issued by that same court and replacing it with a different result. A lower court cannot overrule a precedent from a higher court, however. And because *stare decisis* is a well respected principle, cases are rarely overruled even by the courts that decided them. In general, the Supreme Court will overrule a previous decision only if it is inconsistent with more recent cases, few people have relied on it (possibly because it is a recent decision), or the precedent has become harmful rather than helpful.[17] Here are some of the rare cases where the Supreme Court has overruled its earlier decisions.

> When it is finally time to decide a constitutional issue—or any other legal issue—the lower courts must follow the decisions of the courts above them.

West Virginia State Board of Education v. Barnette (1943)[18]

West Virginia required all public school children to begin the day with a salute to the American flag. Some Jehovah's Witnesses believed that participating in the flag salute violated God's command not to bow down to or worship graven images, so they challenged the requirement. The state thought it was on solid ground because the Supreme Court had upheld a similar requirement in 1940.[19]

This time, however, the Supreme Court reached a different result and overruled the case it had decided just three years earlier. Justices Black and Douglas were part of the difference. As Justice Black stated in a concurring opinion joined by Justice Douglas:

> Reluctance to make the Federal Constitution a rigid bar against state regulation of conduct thought inimical to the public welfare was the controlling influence which moved us to consent to the Gobitis decision. Long reflection convinced us that although the principle is sound, its application in the particular case was wrong. We believe that the statute before us fails to accord full scope to the freedom of religion secured to the appellees by the First and Fourteenth Amendments.[20]

In other words, after "long reflection," Justices Black and Douglas concluded that they were wrong in the earlier case. They also felt the issue was so critical that it should be decided correctly.

Agostini v. Felton (1997), *Mitchell v. Helms* (2000)[21]
Both of these cases challenged state funding for educational activities occurring in private schools. *Agostini* overruled two 1985 decisions holding that remedial services provided by public school employees to parochial school students on parochial school grounds violated the Establishment Clause, and *Mitchell* overruled a 1975 decision and a 1977 decision holding that loaning educational materials and equipment to private religious schools violated the Establishment Clause. Between those earlier cases and *Agostini* and *Mitchell*, the Supreme Court had ruled that many other types of state aid did not violate the Establishment Clause. Since the 1975, 1977, and 1985 decisions

were inconsistent with the intervening ones, the Supreme Court overruled them.

But what if a court cannot rely on *stare decisis* because the case involves new facts or legal principles? The judge will look for decisions in cases with some of the same elements and will either apply the reasoning in those cases or distinguish them by explaining why the differences between them require a separate analysis. When that separate analysis requires the court to interpret a statute or the Constitution, it uses a new set of rules.

First, courts look at the plain language of the law. If the language is clear, the judge must apply it as written except in the rare case where the plain language is obviously inconsistent with the drafters' intent or the law's purpose.[22] In determining whether the language is clear, the courts normally use the ordinary meaning of the words at the time the language was adopted,[23] assume that every word and phrase is included for a reason,[24] and refuse to add words that are not there.[25]

In *Trustees of Dartmouth College v. Woodward* (1819),[26] Chief Justice Marshall set out a general rule that circumstances that fall within the literal words of a particular clause are usually covered by that clause even if the founders could not have foreseen them.

> It is not enough to say that this particular case was not in the mind of the convention when the article was framed, nor of the American people when it was adopted. It is necessary to go further and to say that, had this particular case been suggested, the language would have been so varied as to exclude it, or it would have been made a special exception. The case, being within the words of the rule, must likewise be within its operation, likewise, unless there be something in the literal construction so obviously absurd or mischievous or repugnant to the general spirit of the instrument as to justify those who expound the constitution in making it an exception.[27]

If the language is ambiguous, however, courts will look at the law's direct legislative history.[28] This is what the individuals who wrote it and voted for it said it meant while they were debating and adopting it. For the First Amendment, the direct legislative history comes from the Congressional records of the debates over the Bill of Rights and from records that show what happened during state ratification.

Finally, if the meaning is still unclear after looking at the actual language and the direct legislative history, courts may look at actions or events that occurred outside of the legislative chambers or in connection with other legislation. The courts use this indirect legislative history as a last resort.

The further the courts have to travel down this hierarchy, the less certain it becomes that their interpretation is consistent with the intent of the people who adopted the law, particularly when the legislative history provides support for several different interpretations. And the U.S. Supreme Court has had to search for the meaning of some sections of the First Amendment—particularly the Establishment Clause—on the very bottom rung.

How would the Supreme Court apply these rules to the hypothetical cases from Chapter 1? And how would it interpret the First Amendment to apply to their particular facts? The answers must wait until later, because they depend on the historical background of the First Amendment and on Supreme Court precedent. That exploration starts in the next chapter.

Question 1: The Supreme Court usually avoids constitutional questions if it can decide the case on other grounds. Is this the right approach? Why or why not?

Question 2: There are only two ways to change the holding in a Supreme Court case interpreting the U.S. Constitution: The people can amend the Constitution, or the Supreme Court can overrule the case. So

how much weight should the Supreme Court give
stare decisis when interpreting the Constitution? Is
it more important for the law to be known or for
the law to be right?

CHAPTER THREE
THE THIRD AMENDMENT
BECOMES THE FIRST

When Congress proposed amendments to the Constitution in 1789 and sent them to the states for ratification, the first amendment dealt with the number of representatives the states could send to Congress; the second amendment limited Congress's ability to vote on its own compensation. The clauses about religion were in the third amendment. So how did the third amendment become the first?

The story starts on September 12, 1787. The delegates to the Constitutional Convention had been meeting in Philadelphia since May and had almost completed their work. The Constitution they drafted was a carefully crafted compromise that succeeded so well it is still virtually intact over two centuries later. But it had very little to say about religious freedom.[1]

After a long summer spent hammering out the details of a new government, the delegates were finally getting ready to go home to their families. But George Mason of Virginia had other ideas. With the Constitution almost completed, he persuaded Elbridge Gerry of Massachusetts to move to form a committee to prepare a bill of rights. Mason then seconded Gerry's motion. Their effort failed, however. They could not even get the delegates from their own states to support them, and the motion was defeated.[2]

The records do not show why the Convention defeated Gerry's motion, but there are clues in Roger Sherman's response. Sherman, who was from Connecticut, stated, in effect, that a bill of rights was unnecessary because, "The State Declarations of Rights are not repealed by this Constitution; and being in force are sufficient."[3] Sherman also responded to another motion, two days later, to add a Constitutional provision regarding the freedom of the press. According to Sherman, "It is unnecessary—The power of Congress does not extend to the Press."[4] That motion was also defeated.

So the delegates may have thought a bill of rights was unnecessary. Or they may have been too tired and too homesick to consider matters proposed at the eleventh hour.

The delegates completed their work on September 17, 1787. Thirty of the fifty-five delegates signed the Constitution, with Mason's and Gerry's signatures among the missing. And so the Constitution went to the states for ratification without a bill of rights.

Mason left the convention angry and determined to oppose the proposed Constitution. As Madison described in an October 24, 1787 letter to Thomas Jefferson (who was in Paris as Ambassador to France):

> Col. Mason left Philada. in an exceedingly ill humour indeed. A number of little circumstances arising in part from the impatience which prevailed towards the close of the business conspired to whet his acrimony. He returned to Virginia with a fixed disposition to prevent the adoption of the plan if possible. He considers the want of a Bill of Rights as a fatal objection.[5]

The United States Constitution arose as a phoenix from the ashes of a failed Confederation. Although the Articles of Confederation loosely bound the states together for international purposes, the Confederation had no power to tax, to raise a military, or to enforce its own treaties. It also had no power to prevent one state from discriminating against citizens of another state, and that discouraged commerce among them.

Madison and the other Federalists wanted a central government with the powers necessary to give it clout in its international dealings and to regulate commerce between the states. The Antifederalists, on the other hand, wanted a weak central government that was unable to interfere with the states' actions. They seemed to reverse their arguments when it came to a bill of rights, however.

The Federalists claimed that a declaration of rights was unnecessary because the Constitution did not give the federal government any authority to interfere with individual rights. Some Federalists even claimed that such a declaration was dangerous because it could expand the powers of the federal government by implying that the government did have that authority. Although the Federalists had successfully fought for a strong central government, they resisted a bill of rights by claiming that the new government would be too weak to need one.

The United States Constitution arose as a phoenix from the ashes of a failed Confederation.

The Antifederalists, on the other hand, argued that a constitution without a bill of rights was fatally flawed. They did not get the weak government they wanted, so they opposed it because it did not contain a bill of rights.

Jefferson was in France when the Constitution and the Bill of Rights were adopted, but he maintained a regular correspondence with Madison, who was its primary drafter. That correspondence reveals each of their positions on the subject.

Like the Federalists, Jefferson supported a strong central government. But like the Antifederalists, he was also a strong supporter of a bill of rights. This position was consistent with his description of himself as a free thinker rather than a member of either party. In fact, he was so opposed to belonging to any party that he said "if I could not go to heaven but with a party, I would not go there at all." Still, he admitted that his thinking was much closer to that of the Federalists than the Antifederalists.[6]

After hearing about the provisions of the proposed Constitution, Jefferson wrote Madison and told him what he liked and disliked about it. In his December 20, 1787 letter, Jefferson stated that he did not like "the omission of a bill of rights providing clearly and without the aid of sophisms for freedom of religion, freedom of the press, protection against standing

armies, restriction against monopolies, the eternal and unre-
mitting force of the habeas corpus laws, and trials by jury in
all matters of fact triable by the laws of the land . . ."[7] He went
on to add that "a bill of rights is what the people are entitled
to against every government on earth, general or particular,
and what no just government should refuse, or rest on infer-
ence."[8] Jefferson believed that it would be best for the country
if the first nine states ratified the Constitution so that the new
government would take effect and the next four refused to join
until a declaration of rights was adopted.[9]

Unlike Jefferson, Madison did not feel strongly about a bill
of rights. He supported it halfheartedly because it had popular
support, but he thought it was unnecessary and would be ineffective even if adopted:

> My own opinion has always been in favor of a bill of rights; provided
> it be so framed as not to imply powers not meant to be included
> in the enumeration. At the same time I have never thought the
> omission a material defect, nor been anxious to supply it even by
> *subsequent* amendment, for any other reason than that it is anxiously
> desired by others.[10]

Madison then provided a long list of reasons why he believed
a bill of rights would be ineffective, and one of those reasons
was that the legislative majority would simply ignore it. In the
long run, however, political necessity—and perhaps Jefferson—convinced Madison to become its champion.

Jefferson did not agree that a bill of rights would be ineffective. He reminded Madison that part of the Supreme Court's
role is to enforce it in the face of legislative tyranny. Or, as Jefferson put it:

> In the arguments in favor of a declaration of rights, you omit one
> which has great weight with me, the legal check which it puts
> into the hands of the judiciary. This is a body, which if rendered
> independent, and kept strictly to their own department merits
> great confidence for their learning and integrity.[11]

It was against this political background that Congress sent the new Constitution to the states for ratification.

State Ratification of the Constitution, 1787–1788

Delaware was the first state to ratify the Constitution, voting unanimously on December 2, 1787. New Jersey and Georgia ratified the Constitution unanimously on December 18, 1787 and January 2, 1788, respectively, and Connecticut ratified it on January 9, 1788. None of these states recommended any changes or additions to the Constitution.

Pennsylvania was the second state to ratify the Constitution, doing so by a 46–3 vote on December 12, 1787. A vocal minority wrote a dissent that included fourteen proposed amendments to the Constitution. The first of the amendments proposed by the dissenters read:

> The right of conscience shall be held inviolable; and neither the legislative, executive nor judicial powers of the United States shall have authority to alter, abrogate or infringe any part of the constitution of the several States, which provide for the preservation of liberty in matters of religion.[12]

Maryland ratified the Constitution on April 26, 1788. The state convention appointed a committee to consider amendments to the Constitution, and the committee prepared a report to the convention. Interestingly, the committee considered and voted against an amendment to safeguard religious liberty. The rejected amendment would have stated: "That there be no national religion established by law; but that all persons be equally entitled to protection in their religious liberty."[13] For reasons that are not explained in the convention records, however, the committee decided not to make its report, and Maryland's notice of ratification did not include any recommended amendments.

New Hampshire ratified the Constitution on June 21, 1788, and it recommended twelve amendments. The eleventh of those amendments stated: "Congress shall make no Laws touching Religion, or to infringe the rights of Conscience."[14]

New Hampshire was the ninth state to ratify the new Constitution, putting it into effect and binding the states that had already ratified it.

Virginia ratified the Constitution on June 25, 1788. The battle for ratification in Virginia was hard fought, and the final vote was 89–79. The Antifederalists, led by Patrick Henry, argued that the convention should not ratify a Constitution that did not contain a bill of rights. The Federalists were better strategists, however, and they won the war over the Constitution by surrendering in the battle over the bill of rights.

Although Madison and the other Federalists continued to believe that a bill of rights was unnecessary, their first priority was to get the Constitution ratified and the new government installed. Therefore, they urged the convention to ratify the Constitution as written, and most threw their support behind adding a bill of rights after ratification. Madison even pledged to sponsor it in the new Congress.

Along with ratification, Virginia recommended a bill of rights and twenty other amendments to the Constitution. The twentieth, and last, provision in the proposed bill of rights stated:

> That religion, or the duty which we owe to our Creator, and the manner of discharging it, can be directed only by reason and conviction, not by force or violence; and therefore all men have an equal, natural, and unalienable right to the free exercise of religion, according to the dictates of conscience, and that no particular religious sect or society ought to be favored or established, by law, in preference to others.[15]

New York ratified the Constitution on July 26, 1788 in a close vote (30–27). Like Virginia, New York recommended both a bill of rights and other amendments to the Constitution. The fourth provision in [New York's] proposed bill of rights stated: "That the People have an equal, natural and unalienable right, freely and peaceably to Exercise their Religion according to the dictates of Conscience, and that no Religious Sect or Society ought to be favoured or established by Law in preference of others."[16]

The fourth provision in [New York's] proposed bill of rights stated: "That the People have an equal, natural and unalienable right, freely and peaceably to Exercise their Religion according to the dictates of Conscience, and that no Religious Sect or Society ought to be favoured or established by Law in preference of others.

Massachusetts and South Carolina also recommended amendments when they ratified the Constitution on February 6 and May 23, 1788, respectively. None of those amendments dealt with religion, however.

North Carolina may have been listening to Jefferson because it forfeited representation in the first Congress and withheld ratification of the Constitution until November 21, 1789—after Congress sent the Bill of Rights to the states. This was intentional; the first North Carolina constitutional convention passed a resolution recommending amendments, but it decided neither to ratify nor reject the Constitution until it was amended to North Carolina's satisfaction. It did, however, suggest language for the proposed amendments. North Carolina's amendments—including the one on religious rights—were nearly identical to Virginia's.[17]

Rhode Island—which had not sent a delegate to the Constitutional Convention—was the last to ratify. Rhode Island did not even call a state ratifying convention until after Congress sent the Bill of Rights to the States.

In the end, eleven States ratified the Constitution without a bill of rights. Three of the ratifying states—New Hampshire, Virginia, and New York—recommended an amendment regarding religion. So did North Carolina, which refused to ratify the Constitution without a bill of rights, and the Pennsylvania dissenters. Although individual delegates to the other state conventions may have had concerns about religious liberty, only these five states officially voiced them.

RATIFYING THE UNITED STATES CONSTITUTION

State	Ratification Date	Vote	Did It Recommend Amendments?	Did It Recommend an Amendment Regarding Religion?
Delaware	December 2, 1787	Unanimous	No	
Pennsylvania	December 12, 1787	46–23	Minority Report	Yes
New Jersey	December 18, 1787	Unanimous	No	
Georgia	January 2, 1788	Unanimous	No	
Connecticut	January 9, 1788	128–40	No	
Massachusetts	February 6, 1788	187–168	Yes	No
Maryland	April 26, 1788	63–11	No	
South Carolina	May 23, 1788	149–73	Yes	No
New Hampshire	June 21, 1788	57–46	Yes	Yes
Virginia	June 25, 1788	89–79	Yes	Yes
New York	July 26, 1788	30–27	Yes	Yes
North Carolina	November, 1789	195–77	Yes	Yes
Rhode Island	May 29, 1790	34–32	(No Action)	

The Bill of Rights in the First Congress, 1789

The Federalists had pledged to support a bill of rights they thought unnecessary. Once the states ratified the Constitution, the Antifederalists also switched sides and argued that a bill of rights was not a priority for the new government. They may have hoped the states would be so dissatisfied that they would call another constitutional convention and scrap the new government altogether.

James Madison, Elbridge Gerry, and Roger Sherman were all elected to serve in the new House of Representatives. The House convened on March 4, 1789, but, in the days before automobiles and routine road maintenance, it was April 1 before enough representatives arrived to make a quorum.

Madison kept his promise. On June 8, 1789, he proposed a bill of rights. He did not argue that a bill of rights was necessary in its own right—which he still did not believe—but only that Congress should keep its promise to the people who relied on it in ratifying the Constitution. He also used Jefferson's argument that the judicial branch would protect the bill of rights from becoming ineffective.

> If [a bill of rights is] incorporated into the constitution, independent
> tribunals of justice will consider themselves in a peculiar manner
> the guardians of those rights; they will be an impenetrable bulwark
> against every assumption of power in the legislative or executive;
> they will be naturally led to resist every encroachment upon rights
> expressly stipulated for in the constitution by the declaration of
> rights.[18]

Although the House kept an official record of its proceedings, the *House of Representatives Journal* merely records the matters considered by the House, the actions it took, and the vote. It does not include the debates. The debates are recorded in the *Annals of Congress,* which were compiled approximately fifty years later from the best records available at the time, including contemporary newspaper accounts. Since speeches were paraphrased rather than quoted verbatim, there is no guarantee that they are accurate. Still, the *Annals of Congress* is the best source available for the Congressional debates.

Unlike the debates, proposed language was faithfully recorded. In regard to religious rights, Madison's proposed language read:

> The civil rights of none shall be abridged on account of religious
> belief or worship, nor shall any national religion be established,
> nor shall the full and equal rights of conscience be in any manner,
> or on any pretext, infringed.[19]

The House referred the proposal to a select committee composed of one member from each of the eleven states that had ratified the Constitution and were represented in Congress. On August 13 the select committee reported it to the whole House. The select committee made few substantive changes to Madison's proposal but did shorten the provision regarding religious rights to read: "No religion shall be established by law, nor shall the equal rights of conscience be infringed."[20]

Gerry's response to the select committee's report illustrates the Antifederalists' new strategy. According to the *Annals of Congress,* "Mr. Gerry thought the discussion would take up more

time than the House could now spare," and he wanted to table
the report until after Congress considered other matters.[21]

The Antifederalists were in the minority, however, and the
House began debating the language in the proposal. It reached
the fourth proposition on August 15.

The most significant debate about the religion clause—at
least as recorded in the *Annals of Congress*—occurred on that
day. Here are some highlights:

- Peter Sylvester of New York was afraid it would abolish
  religious practice altogether.
- Gerry wanted it to say, "No religious doctrine shall be
  established by law."
- Sherman, who—unlike many of the other Federalists—had not changed his stand since the Constitutional Convention, thought the amendment was unnecessary because Congress did not have authority to
  establish religion.
- When asked what the clause meant, "Mr. Madison said,
  he apprehended the meaning of the words to be, that
  Congress should not establish a religion, and enforce
  the legal observation of it by law, nor compel men to
  worship God in any manner contrary to their conscience."[22]
- Benjamin Huntington of Connecticut was concerned
  that the amendment would prohibit paying for ministers or church buildings, and he did not want it to
  protect anyone who professed no religion at all.

The full debate is included in Appendix A.

The House amended the language several times, reorganized
the Bill of Rights so that it came at the end of the Constitution
rather than changing the existing text, and passed the amendments on August 24. When the House sent the Bill of Rights
to the Senate, the fourth proposition had become the third
article and read as follows:

> 3. Congress shall make no law establishing religion, or prohibiting the free exercise thereof; nor shall the rights of conscience be infringed.[23]

The Senate met behind closed doors for its first few years, so its debates on the Bill of Rights are lost to history. The *Senate Journal* records the actions taken and little else, and the *Annals of Congress* are virtually useless.

On September 2, 1789, the Senate began considering the Bill of Rights. It amended the third article on September 3 and again on September 9 before adopting it. As adopted, the third article now read:

> Congress shall make no law establishing articles of faith, or a mode of worship, or prohibiting the free exercise of religion, or abridging the freedom of speech, or the press, or the right of the people peaceably to assemble, and petition to the government for the redress of grievances.[24]

Since the Senate version was not identical to the House version, the two houses of Congress met in conference to agree on the language of the third article. The House adopted the conference language on September 24, and the Senate adopted it on September 25.

The final version of the third article, as proposed by Congress and sent to the states for ratification, read as follows:

> **Article III.** Congress shall make no law respecting an establishment of religion, or prohibiting the free exercise thereof; or abridging the freedom of speech, or of the press, or the right of the people peaceably to assemble, and to petition the Government for a redress of grievances.[25]

Language Changes in the Religion Clauses

Date	Text
June 8, 1789 (House)	The civil rights of none shall be abridged on account of religious belief or worship, nor shall any national religion be established, nor shall the full and equal rights of conscience be in any manner, or on any pretext infringed. [As introduced.]
August 13 (House)	No religion shall be established by law, nor shall the equal rights of conscience be infringed.
August 15 (House)	Congress shall make no laws touching religion, or infringing the rights of conscience.
August 20 (House)	Congress shall make no law establishing religion, or to prevent the free exercise thereof; or to infringe the rights of conscience.
August 24 (House)	Congress shall make no law establishing religion, or prohibiting the free exercise thereof; nor shall the rights of conscience be infringed. [Sent to the Senate.]
September 3 (Senate)	Congress shall make no law establishing religion, or prohibiting the free exercise thereof.
September 9 (Senate)	Congress shall make no law establishing aricles of faith, or a mode of worship, or prohibiting the free exercise of religion, or abridging the freedom of speech, or the press, or the right of the people peaceably to assemble, and petition to the government for the redress of grievances. [Sent back to the House.]
September 24 (House)	Congress shall make no law respecting an establishment of religion, or prohibiting the free exercise thereof; or abridging the freedom of speech, or of the press, or the right of the people peaceably to assemble, and to petition the Government for a redress of grievances. [Final version.]
September 25 (Senate)	[Same.]

The Bill of Rights in the States, 1789–1791

When the Bill of Rights went to the states for ratification, it had twelve amendments.

- The first amendment dealt with the number of representatives each state could elect to Congress;
- The second amendment provided that Congress could not give itself a raise or take a pay cut unless it took effect after the next election;
- The third amendment was the current First Amendment; and
- The fourth through twelfth amendments were the current Second through Tenth Amendments.

This time the states did not call ratifying conventions. Instead, the state legislatures voted on ratification.

During 1789 and 1790, nine states ratified the current ten amendments. Maryland, North Carolina, and South Carolina ratified all twelve amendments. New Hampshire, New Jersey, New York, and Rhode Island ratified the first amendment and the third through twelfth amendments but not the second. Delaware ratified all except the first amendment, and Pennsylvania ratified the third through twelfth amendments but not the first and second.

The reports on the states' ratification efforts are very sketchy and come mostly from newspaper articles and letters. The most detailed accounts cover the controversy in Virginia, where what is now the First Amendment ran into trouble.

The Virginia House initially disagreed about several amendments (not including the third), but the House resolved its internal dispute and sent all twelve amendments to the Virginia Senate. The Senate objected to the third amendment, among others, but the sources do not explain why.

The Virginia Federalists then tabled the amendments. They believed that most Virginians supported the amendments, so they let an election intervene. Their tactic succeeded, and Virginia ratified all twelve amendments on December 15, 1791.[26]

Vermont, which became a state on March 4, 1791, also ratified all twelve amendments. Massachusetts, Connecticut, and
Georgia had not ratified any of the amendments by the end
of the Second Congress. As a result, the first two amendments
failed, and the third became the first.[27]

STATES RATIFYING THE BILL OF RIGHTS

State	All Twelve Amendments	All Except the First Amendment	All Except the Second Amendment	The Last Ten Amendments
Connecticut	(Absent)			
Delaware		X		
Georgia	(Absent)			
Maryland	X			
Massachusetts	(Absent)			
New Hampshire			X	
New Jersey			X	
New York			X	
North Carolina	X			
Pennsylvania				X
Rhode Island			X	
South Carolina	X			
Vermont	X			
Virginia	X			

The only thing that is clear from the direct legislative history
is that Justice Jackson got it wrong in *Everson v. Board of Education* when he said, "This freedom was first in the Bill of Rights
because it was first in the forefathers' minds . . . ."[28] The First
Amendment's position in the Bill of Rights is purely an acci-
dent of history. It was third among the amendments sent to
the states for ratification and achieved its current position only
because the first two amendments were not ratified. Earlier,
when the states ratified the Constitution, only four of them
and the dissenting minority from Pennsylvania recommended
adding an amendment regarding religious freedom, and only
the Pennsylvania dissent placed it first on the list. In fact, it was
dead last in the bill of rights proposed by Virginia and North
Carolina. While the First Amendment has become first in importance to modern-day Americans, it may not have held that
lofty status with the founding fathers.

Question 1: The founding fathers used the word "religion" in the First Amendment instead of the word "Christianity." Does their choice of words affect the amendment's meaning? How?

Question 2: Based on the First Amendment's direct legislative history, what do you think the first Congress meant when it prohibited laws "respecting an establishment of religion"?

CHAPTER FOUR
ONCE UPON A TIME

In May 1776, a young and politically inexperienced James Madison was a delegate to a convention called to adopt a declaration of rights and a plan of government for Virginia. George Mason drafted the Virginia Declaration of Rights, and Madison stayed in the background. Except on one issue. According to his autobiography, Madison suggested the religion clause be modified by replacing the word "toleration" with a phrase that "declared the freedom of conscience to be a *natural and absolute* right."[1] The delegates accepted Madison's change, and his political career began on a high note.Theoretically, a constitutional amendment means what the people who adopted it thought it meant at the time. For the religion clauses of the First Amendment, the best place to discover that intent is from the debates in Congress and the state ratifying bodies, which were discussed in the last chapter. Since those debates do not provide a clear answer, however, the courts look at other events that may shine some light on its meaning. This indirect legislative history deserves less weight, however, because there is no guarantee that it shines the light on the right places.

The First Amendment's indirect legislative history comes from its political and religious setting, the writings of men such as Madison and Jefferson, and Congress's actions around the time the First Amendment was adopted. Whole books have been written about the religious history of the American colonies, but that is not the focus of this one. It is enough to say that, in 1776, the vast majority of people living in America considered themselves Protestant Christians—Episcopalian, Congregationalist, Baptist, Presbyterian, or Quaker, among others. There were a smaller number of Catholic Christians, a handful of Jews, and an occassional atheist.[2]

On May 10, 1776, the Second Continental Congress recommended that each state adopt its own constitution.[3] Virginia was one of the first to act. Delegates to the Virginia convention appointed a drafting committee on May 15 and adopted a declaration of rights on June 12. It read:

> 16. That Religion, or the duty which we owe to our Creator, and
> the manner of discharging it, can be directed only by reason and
> conviction, not by force or violence; and, therefore, all men are
> equally entitled to the free exercise of religion, according to the
> dictates of conscience; and that it is the mutual duty of all to practise
> Christian forbearance, love, and charity towards each other.[4]

The other states quickly followed with their own declarations
of rights, although some incorporated them into the body of
the constitution. Most were not as expansive as Virginia's, however.

Georgia had the most liberal clause. Its constitution stated:
"All persons whatever shall have the free exercise of their religion; provided it be not repugnant to the peace and safety of
the State; and shall not, unless by consent, support any teacher
or teachers except those of their own profession."[5] New York
also used the word "religion" without referring to God, the
Creator, or a Supreme Being. On the other hand, New York's
constitution prohibited ministers from holding public office
since that could distract them from their religious duties.[6]

North Carolina adopted a declaration of rights with a very
short free exercise clause. It simply said, "That all men have
a natural and unalienable right to worship Almighty God according to the dictates of their own consciences."[7]

Delaware's and Pennsylvania's declarations of rights both
said that all men have the right to worship "Almighty God" as
their consciences dictate, although Delaware gave equal rights
and privileges only to Christians.[8] Pennsylvania provided that
no man who "acknowledges the being of a God" could be deprived of his civil rights based on his religion, but it required
public officeholders to take an oath that they believed in the
God of both the Old and New Testaments—essentially requiring them to be Christians.[9]

Maryland's declaration of rights contained four long clauses
regarding religious rights and obligations. It gave freedom of
worship and equal rights to Christians and expressly gave the
Maryland legislature power to tax its citizens to support Chris-

tianity, although each individual had the right to decide which Christian denomination would benefit from his taxes.[10]

New Jersey's constitution provided that no person should "be deprived of the inestimable privilege of worshiping Almighty God in a manner agreeable to the dictates of his own conscience" or be compelled to attend worship "contrary to his own faith and judgment" or be required to pay taxes or other fees to build any church or support any ministry. It also provided that "there shall be no establishment of any one religious sect in this Province, in preference to another" and that Protestants could not be deprived of their civil rights merely because of the sect they belonged to.[11]

Massachusetts and New Hampshire had similar requirements. The first of two clauses in the Massachusetts declaration of rights said that it was everyone's duty to worship the "Supreme Being" but that no one should be harmed for worshiping God according to his own beliefs. The second clause was the subject of long debate. The first paragraph of the final version read:

> As the happiness of a people, and the good order and preservation of civil government essentially depend upon piety, religion and morality, and as these cannot be generally diffused through a community, but by the institution of the public worship of God, and of public instructions in piety, religion and morality: Therefore, to promote their happiness and to secure the good order and preservation of their government, the people of this Commonwealth have a right to invest their legislature with power to authorize and require, and the legislature shall, from time to time, authorize and require, the several towns, parishes, precincts, and other bodies-politic, or religious societies, to make suitable provision, at their own expense, for the institution of the public worship of God, and for the support and maintenance of public protestant teachers of piety, religion and morality, in all cases where such provision shall not be made voluntarily.[12]

Massachusetts's declaration of rights did allow its citizens to direct their assessment to a particular Protestant group if they regularly attended its worship services. Anyone who did not attend regularly still had to pay but did not get any say in which group received the money. Massachusetts and New Hampshire also gave all Christians a right to equal protection under the laws.[13]

Vermont set up its own government and adopted a declaration of rights before the end of 1777 even though it had not been a separate colony and did not become a state until 1791. Vermont provided full civil rights for Protestants and freedom of worship for all who believed in "Almighty God." Vermont encouraged worship, however, by stating that "every sect or denomination of people ought to observe the Sabbath, or the Lord's day, and keep up, and support, some sort of religious worship, which to them shall seem most agreeable to the revealed will of God."[14]

South Carolina's constitution was the most restrictive and established Protestantism as the state's official religion. The constitution required the governor, lieutenant governor, members of a privy counsel, and all of the legislators to be Protestants and prohibited ministers from holding public office.[15] A very long article dealt with religious rights and began as follows:

> That all persons and religious societies who acknowledge that there is one God, and a future state of rewards and punishments, and that God is publicly to be worshipped, shall be freely tolerated. The Christian Protestant religion shall be deemed, and is hereby constituted and declared to be, the established religion of this State. That all denominations of Christian Protestants in this State, demeaning themselves peaceably and faithfully, shall enjoy equal religious and civil privileges.[16]

Finally, Connecticut's short declaration of rights did not contain any provision guaranteeing religious freedom. It did, however, mention religion in the preamble, stating that "forasmuch as the free Fruition of such Liberties and Privileges as Humanity, Civility and Christianity call for, as is due to every Man in his Place and Proportion . . . hath ever been, and will be the Tranquility and Stability of Churches and Commonwealths."[17]

So what do these state declarations say about the mindset of the men who would later draft the First Amendment? They all believed in religious freedom, but they did not agree about what that meant.

In some states, full religious freedom was just for Protestants, while in others it was for everyone. Jews appear to have fared best in Virginia, Georgia, North Carolina, and New York. Catholics were discriminated against in New Jersey, Massachusetts, New Hampshire, and Vermont and could not even hold office in South Carolina.

So what do these state declarations say about the mindset of the men who would later draft the First Amendment? They all believed in religious freedom, but they did not agree about what that meant.

Madison's and Jefferson's writings can also shed light on the meaning of the First Amendment's religion clauses. They must be viewed with caution, however, since some were written about a state fight for religious freedom, not a federal one, and the others were written long after the First Amendment was adopted.

The Quest for Religious Freedom in Virginia

The Virginia legislature considered a bill to support Christian teachers in 1785—four years before Congress considered the First Amendment. Madison opposed the bill, which was sponsored by one of his biggest political foes, Patrick Henry (then governor of Virginia).[18] Madison's "Memorial and Remonstrance Against Religious Assessments" gave fifteen reasons why no government should dictate a person's religion or force anyone to support a religion he disagreed with. Several of those reasons provide insight into Madison's position on what religions and religious activities should be protected from government interference.

3. ...Who does not see that the same authority which can establish Christianity, in exclusion of all other Religions, may establish with the same ease any particular sect of Christians, in exclusion of all other Sects? That the same authority which can force a citizen to contribute three pence only of his property for the support of any one establishment, may force him to conform to any other establishment in all cases whatsoever?

4. ...Whilst we assert for ourselves a freedom to embrace, to profess and to observe the Religion which we believe to be of divine origin, we cannot deny an equal freedom to those whose minds have not yet yielded to the evidence which has convinced us. If this freedom be abused, it is an offence against God, not against man: To God, therefore, not to man, must an account of it be rendered.

8. ... a Government will be best supported by protecting every Citizen in the enjoyment of his Religion with the same equal hand which protects his person and his property; by neither invading the equal rights of any Sect, nor suffering any Sect to invade those of another.[19]

The full text of the "Memorial and Remonstrance" is included as Appendix B.

Jefferson had drafted "The Virginia Act for Establishing Religious Freedom" several years earlier. Virginia did not pass it before Jefferson left for France, however, so Madison took over as its sponsor. Madison convinced the legislature to adopt the Act in 1786, just months after his "Memorial and Remonstrance" defeated the assessment for Christian teachers. The text of the Act is quite specific:

That no man shall be compelled to frequent or support any religious worship, place, or ministry whatsoever, nor shall be enforced, restrained, molested, or burthened in his body or goods, nor shall otherwise suffer on account of his religious opinions or belief; but that all men shall be free to profess, and by argument to maintain, their opinion in matters of religion, and that the same shall in no wise diminish, enlarge, or affect their civil capacities.[20]

Some of the members of the Virginia legislature attempted to limit the bill's protections to Christians.[21] Their attempt failed, however.

"A Wall of Separation"

In 1801, a decade after the states ratified the Bill of Rights, President Jefferson received a letter from the Danbury Baptist Association.[22] The letter congratulated him on his election and requested his help to persuade state governments to stop legislating about religion.

Jefferson responded on January 1, 1802.[23] One phrase in his letter—"a wall of separation between church and state"—has been quoted in several Supreme Court opinions to support the proposition that the First Amendment prohibits the federal government from supporting religious organizations in any way.[24] The entire sentence reads:

> Believing with you that religion is a matter which lies solely between Man & his God, that he owes account to none other for his faith or his worship, that the legitimate powers of government reach actions only, & not opinions, I contemplate with sovereign reverence that act of the whole American people which declared that their legislature should "make no law respecting an establishment of religion, or prohibiting the free exercise thereof," thus building a wall of separation between Church & State.[25]

The Danbury Baptists were Jefferson's allies, but he apparently thought about using his reply as a public attack on his political enemies. Those enemies called Jefferson an infidel because he refused to issue proclamations for public days of fasting and thanksgiving. In a draft of his letter, Jefferson identified those proclamations as a British practice, which would have angered his political enemies by associating them with the hated monarchy. Cooler heads prevailed, however, and Jefferson's letter was toned down before it was sent.[26]

Madison also used the word "separation" to describe the religion clauses. In the "Detached Memoranda" written sometime after he retired from public life, Madison characterized the First Amendment as a provision that "strongly guarded ... the separation between Religion & Govt in the Constitution of the United States."[27]

Do Jefferson's metaphor of "a wall of separation between church and state" and Madison's statement that the Bill of Rights strongly guards that separation accurately describe Congress's and the states' intent when adopting the First Amendment? Or was Jefferson's metaphor just a political phrase meant to appease his allies and answer his critics? And was Madison's statement colored by the passing years and a fading memory? Unfortunately, there is no way to know for sure.

Another source of indirect legislative history comes from the contemporaneous actions of the men who adopted the First Amendment. In particular, the actions taken by Congress around the same time may provide some clues to what it intended the First Amendment to mean.

On May 1, 1789, just a few months before approving the Bill of Rights, the House of Representatives elected a House chaplain.[28] On March 3, 1791, the same Representatives who had approved the First Amendment enacted a bill adding another regiment to the military and authorizing it to hire a military chaplain with a monthly salary of $50.[29] Apparently the majority of the members of the House did not believe the First Amendment prohibited them from appointing a chaplain to open their daily sessions or paying a military chaplain from public funds.

In later years, Madison objected to appointing chaplains. As he stated in his "Detached Memoranda":

> Is the appointment of Chaplains to the two Houses of Congress consistent with the Constitution, and with the pure principle of religious freedom?
>
> In strictness the answer on both points must be in the negative. The Constitution of the U.S. forbids everything like an

> establishment of a national religion. The law appointing Chaplains establishes a religious worship for the national representatives, to be performed by Ministers of religion, elected by a majority of them; and these are to be paid out of the national taxes. Does not this involve the principle of a national establishment, applicable to a provision for a religious worship for the Constituent as well as of the representative Body, approved by the majority, and conducted by Ministers of religion paid by the entire nation.[30]

Madison also objected to military chaplains for similar reasons.[31]

Although Madison claimed that appointing chaplains violated the Establishment Clause, it is the intent of Congress, as represented by the adopting majority, rather than the intent of the drafter that matters. Furthermore, there is no official record of Madison objecting to the House's actions when they occurred. And, even in his later years, he at least tolerated the idea of Congressional chaplains paid for by "voluntary contribution from the members."[32]

So what conclusions does the indirect legislative history produce? Many of the state declarations of rights would lead one to believe that the statesmen of the time only wanted to protect Christians—and only Protestant Christians, at that. The Congressional actions approving the use of chaplains support this interpretation. On the other hand, Madison's writings make it clear that he wanted to protect everyone's religious freedom, including "those whose minds have not yet yielded to the evidence which has convinced [Christians]," and Jefferson's letter to the Danbury Baptists supports that interpretation.[33] So where does the legislative history—direct and indirect—lead?

Many of the state declarations of rights would lead one to believe that the statesmen of the time only wanted to protect Christians—and only Protestant Christians, at that.

The meaning of the First Amendment—and the Establishment Clause in particular—is as clear as the buildings on the
other side of the street in a blizzard. Some of the legislative history blows the snow to the right and some of it blows the snow
to the left, but none of it blows the snow away. That leaves the
Supreme Court Justices with the unenviable task of exercising
their own best judgment as to what the founders meant. And,
as subsequent chapters will show, intelligent men and women
can, and do, disagree.

Question 1: Based on the language in the state declarations of
rights, do you think the states ratifying the First
Amendment agreed on what it meant? If so, what
did it mean to them? If not, how should the courts
reconcile those divergent views?

Question 2: What did Thomas Jefferson mean when he told the
Danbury Baptist Association that the First Amend-
ment creates "a wall of separation between Church
& State"? How much weight should the courts give
his statement when interpreting the Establishment
Clause?

CHAPTER FIVE

THE SILENT AMENDMENT

The Supreme Court was silent about the First Amendment's religion clauses during the first 100 years after the Bill of Rights was
adopted. Then it decided several Mormon polygamy cases in the
late 1800s that raised the Free Exercise Clause.[1] It also decided
a 1908 Free Exercise case that challenged paying for Catholic
education from funds held for the benefit of the Sioux as part of
a treaty.[2] Then First Amendment religion cases took a hiatus until
the late 1930s.[3]

There were religion cases during these two periods, however.
The Court heard its first one in 1815 and continued to hear them
all along. But the First Amendment lay dormant during most of
the nineteenth century and the beginning of the twentieth.

So what cases did the Court decide during these silent periods?

Land Ownership

What if two entities claim to own the same land? And does it
make a difference if one of them is a church? Here are several
cases that addressed that issue.

Terrett v. Taylor (1815)[4]

As a colony, Virginia had an official church—the Episcopal
Church (also known as the Anglican Church or the Church
of England)—but after the Revolutionary War it got a divorce.
Although the state legislature first confirmed the right of Episcopal parishes to own land, it later declared that all land belonging to the Episcopal Church now belonged to the county it
was located in for the use of the poor. The legislature claimed
that its action was required by the Virginia Constitution's free
exercise clause.

Terrett v. Taylor involved an Episcopal parish that had originally been located entirely in Virginia. Episcopal parishes were

defined geographically, and when the United States created the District of Columbia, part of the parish ended up in D.C. and part remained in Virginia.

The parish had used its own funds to purchase property before the war, and now the Vestry (the parish leaders) wanted to sell the unused land and apply the proceeds to church business. Unfortunately for them, officials in Fairfax County, Virginia, claimed the land and its proceeds for poor relief.

This case occurred long before the Fourteenth Amendment was adopted. Since the church's dispute was with Virginia, not the federal government, the U.S. Supreme Court could not have decided it under the First Amendment even if it wanted to. Instead, it looked at general principles of land ownership, weighed the equities, and concluded that the state could not seize land merely because it belonged to a church.

The justices also concluded that the Virginia constitution did not require the legislature to deprive Episcopal parishes of the right to own land. As Justice Story noted:

> Consistent with the constitution of Virginia the legislature could not create or continue a religious establishment which should have exclusive rights and prerogatives, or compel the citizens to worship under a stipulated form or discipline, or to pay taxes to those whose creed they could not conscientiously believe. But the free exercise of religion cannot be justly deemed to be restrained by aiding with equal attention the votaries of every sect to perform their own religious duties. . . .[5]

Therefore, the Court concluded that the land belonged to the Episcopal parish, which could sell it and use the money any way it wanted.

Mason v. Muncaster (1824)[6]

After winning *Terrett*, the Vestry sold the land to John Mason. Mason bought it for a down payment and promissory notes. When the notes became due, Mason tried to get out of paying them by claiming that the land sale was void because the sale was not made by the right Vestry.

While the Episcopal Church was still Virginia's official church, Virginia law provided that one Vestry—elected by the members of the parish—would manage all of the parish's business. At one point the Fairfax parish had two churches, one in Alexandria (now in D.C.), and one in Falls Church (still in Virginia). Falls Church fell into disrepair, and the parish stopped holding services there. The Alexandria church had members from both Virginia and D.C., and the members of the Alexandria church elected the Vestry that sold Mason the land.

For years, no one attempted to elect a separate Falls Church Vestry. Then, in 1819, a group of people who claimed to belong to that church elected one. Mason argued that the Falls Church Vestry was the parish's true Vestry, and the sale by the Alexandria Vestry was void.

The Supreme Court made short work of Mason's claim. It noted that Falls Church had fallen into disrepair and that the Alexandria church had been the only worshiping church in the parish for many years. It also found that the members of the Alexandria church—which included residents of Virginia as well as D.C.—had treated it and the Vestry they chose as the only one for many years. As a result, the Court held that the land purchase was valid and Mason was responsible for the remaining purchase price.

Ponce v. Roman Catholic Apostolic Church (1908)[7]
The question the Supreme Court answered in *Terrett* was asked again almost a century later. Before the United States took possession of Puerto Rico, the ruling Spanish government recognized the Roman Catholic Church as Puerto Rico's official church. It had a separate corporate existence and the right to own property. Some of the funds to purchase that property came from private donors, and some may have come from public funds.

When Puerto Rico became an American territory, the City of Ponce tried to seize the church property located within its borders, claiming it was purchased with public funds. The Supreme Court did not care where the funds originally came from, however. They were given to the Roman Catholic Church without any conditions or restrictions, so the funds and the property purchased with them belonged to the Church.

Missionary Society of M.E. Church v. Dalles City (1883)[8]
The Missionary Society for the Methodist Episcopal Church wanted to bring the Gospel to the American Indians, so around 1836 it established a missionary station in what later became Dalles City, Oregon. The Society ran the station until 1847, when it decided it was spread too thin and did not have the funds to maintain the mission. So it transferred the station to Dr. Whitman of the Presbyterian Missionary Society.

Dr. Whitman left the missionary station in the charge of his 17-year-old nephew, Perrin, and returned to his home about 140 miles away. Approximately two months later, Dr. Whitman and his family were murdered by the Cayuse Indians. Upon hearing the news, Perrin abandoned the missionary station and left the area. The mission remained abandoned, and the land eventually became part of Dalles City.

On August 14, 1848, Congress passed a law establishing Oregon as a territory. The law gave missionary societies up to 640 acres of the land they were occupying at the time for the use and benefit of the Indians. The Presbyterian Missionary Society gave up all claim to the station in favor of the Methodist Missionary Society, and that Society decided to take advantage of Congress's action and claim the land where the station stood.

Sometime after August 14, 1848, and before the Society made its claim known, Dalles City filed a claim with the land office and paid for the property. So who owned the land?

The Court said Dalles City did. Congress had only granted title to missionary societies that were occupying the land at the time for the use and benefit of the Indians. The station at Dalles City had been voluntarily abandoned before then. The Society had no right to the land, and Dalles City's title was good.

Corporation of the Catholic Bishop of Nesqually v. Gibbon (1895)[9]
The Catholic Bishop of Nesqually tried to take advantage of

the same law. Before Oregon became a territory, the Bishop obtained permission from the Hudson Bay Company to put up a building on land within the Company's complex. The Catholic missionaries used the building as a church and school for the local Indians as well as for other residents. In 1850, the United States purchased the compound from the Hudson Bay Company for use as a military base. The Bishop claimed that the 1848 law gave the mission 640 acres, which included the land the building was on and the surrounding area. The Secretary of the Interior agreed to the Church's title to the small parcel of land the building sat on but not to the remaining land, which had never been in the Church's possession or control.

The Court looked at the language in the Act, which gave missionary societies "up to" 640 acres of land occupied or used by a missionary society. The Catholic missionaries had not occupied or even used any of the land except where the building stood. The law did not give every missionary society 640 acres, and the Bishop had to be content with what the mission had already received.

Communal Property

Can individuals agree to give their property and wages to a religious society in exchange for the society's commitment to take care of them? The Court has consistently answered the question in the affirmative. The following cases are just a sample.

Goesele v. Bimeler (1852)[10]

Joseph Bimeler and Johannes Goesele were members of the Society of Separatists. They and other Separatists emigrated from Germany in 1817 to escape religious persecution. When they reached America, Bimeler, who was the group's leader, purchased 5,500 acres of land in Ohio in his own name, with the purchase price to be paid over time. The Separatists were assigned their own tracts of land to farm, and they eventually paid off the debt and accumulated another 10,000 acres through their joint labors.

Apparently the original plan was for the members of the community to own the land they farmed, but they soon realized their plan would not work because many of them were too frail to farm. So, in 1819, all the members signed an agreement giving up their individual rights to the property and assigning it all to the Society. In return, the Society agreed to take care of their needs at all times—including when they were sick or elderly and unable to work.

The Separatists were hard workers, and the community was very prosperous. Between Goesele's death in 1827 and the time the case reached the Supreme Court, the property's value had increased 700 percent. And his heirs wanted a share. They wanted not only the land Goesele had been assigned when the group arrived in Ohio, but also a proportionate share of everything the community had earned since then. They got none of it.

The Court found that Goesele and the other members of the community voluntarily gave up their right to own property in exchange for the right to be cared for during their lifetimes (or until they voluntarily left the community). They knew what they were giving up, and the Court thought it was a fair bargain.

Baker v. Nachtrieb (1856)[11]
The Harmony Society had a similar arrangement. Formed by another group of German immigrants under the leadership of George Rapp, the Society settled in Pennsylvania in 1805, moved to Indiana in 1814, and returned to Pennsylvania in 1825. The Harmony Society believed in holding all things in common, as the early Christians had done.

Joshua Nachtrieb joined the Society in Indiana in 1819. He signed its standard documents giving up the right to any property or payment for his labor and services. In exchange, the Society agreed to care for him for the rest of his life or until he left. If he left the society, Rapp could—but did not have to—give him some of the Society's money to help him start life outside the community.

By 1846, Nachtrieb became unhappy and decided to leave. He asked Rapp for money, and Rapp gave him $200 in exchange for a written acknowledgement that he had withdrawn from the Society.

Nachtrieb took the money and left. Then he sued for more, claiming that Rapp had forced him to leave and forfeit his share of the property purchased with the fruits of his labors.

As with the Separatists, the Court ruled that the members of the Harmony Society had voluntarily given up their rights to money or property in exchange for a promise to be cared for as long as they were members of the Society. The Court also found that Rapp had not done anything improper to cause Nachtrieb to leave. In fact, Nachtrieb was lucky to get the $200.

Order of St. Benedict of New Jersey v. Steinhauser (1914) [12]
Augustin Wirth was a priest who belonged to the Order of St. Benedict. The members agreed to give all of their property and individual earnings to the Order while they belonged to it and to keep only what they needed to support themselves. Father Wirth was over seventy and still a member of the Order when he died.

Father Wirth was also an author. He wrote a number of books on religious subjects and continued to receive royalties after his death. His publishers paid the royalties to the Order until the administrator of his estate claimed them.[13] Then it was up to the courts to decide who owned the copyright: the Order or Father Wirth's heirs.

The Abbot who headed the Order had allowed Father Wirth to receive the royalties during his lifetime, so the administrator argued that he owned the property when he died. The Supreme Court found, however, that the Abbot let Father Wirth receive the money so that he could decide what charitable uses it would go to—not because Father Wirth owned the copyrights. The copyrights belonged to the Order, as did everything else Father Wirth had the use of, and it got the royalties.

Education

In the early twentieth century, the religion cases began focusing on the relationship between state laws and parochial schools. Although the Fourteenth Amendment had been in effect for more than fifty years, the Supreme Court did not use it to apply the First Amendment's religion clauses to the states until the 1930s. The Court also heard a case in the mid-1800s that directly involved religious education—or the lack of it. Those cases follow.

Vidal v. Philadelphia (1844)[14]

Stephen Girard died wealthy. He had several nieces and nephews but no sons or daughters, so he chose to leave his money to Philadelphia for a college for orphans. His will contained detailed instructions for running the school, including the following:

> I enjoin and require that no ecclesiastic, missionary, or minister of any sect whatsoever, shall ever hold or exercise any station or duty whatever in the said college; nor shall any such person ever be admitted for any purpose, or as a visitor, within the premises appropriated to the purposes of the said college.
>
> In making this restriction, I do not mean to cast any reflection upon any sect or persons whatsoever; but, as there is such a multitude of sects, and such a diversity of opinion amongst them, I desire to keep the tender minds of the orphans, who are to derive advantage from this bequest, free from the excitement which clashing doctrines and sectarian controversy are so apt to produce; ...[15]

Girard's nieces and nephews thought he should have left the money to them rather than to Philadelphia. Since they would get the money if he died without a will, they asked the courts to invalidate it. One of their arguments was that the conditions banning religious personnel were hostile to Christianity, so the will was against Pennsylvania's public policy and void.

Justice Story's opinion for the Court looked at Pennsylvania's constitution to apply its public policy.

> The constitution of 1790 ... expressly declares, "That all men have a natural and indefeasible right to worship Almighty God according to the dictates of their own consciences; no man can of right be compelled to attend, erect, or support any place of worship, or to maintain any ministry against his consent; no human authority can, in any case whatever, control or interfere with the rights of conscience; and no preference shall ever be given by law to any religious establishment or modes of worship." Language more comprehensive for the complete protection of every variety of religious opinion could scarcely be used; and it must have been intended to extend equally to all sects, whether they believed in Christianity or not, and whether they were Jews or infidels.[16]

Against this background, the opinion asked, "Is an omission to provide for instruction in Christianity in any scheme of school or college education a fatal defect, which avoids it according to the law of Pennsylvania?"[17] The Court answered the question "no" and held that the will was valid. Philadelphia got the money to establish the college, and the nieces and nephews received nothing but legal bills.

Lowrey v. Territory of Hawaii (1907) (1910)[18]
The American Board of Commissioners for Foreign Missions ran several schools in the Hawaiian Islands. One of those schools, located on the Island of Maui, taught both liberal arts and religion classes and prepared some students for the ministry.

By 1850, the school had become the leading educational institution in Hawaii. It was also costing the Board more money to run than the Board of Missions could afford. The Board did not want the Island to lose the school, however, so it offered to give it to the Hawaiian government with conditions. One condition was that the school was not to teach any religious doctrine that was inconsistent with the ones taught by the school when it was run by the mission society. If the government violated the condition, the school's ownership would revert to the Board of Missions.

The government asked that the penalty for violating the condition be changed to give it the option of paying $15,000 instead of losing the school. It also wanted a specific statement of faith so that it would know what doctrine it had to use. The Board of Missions agreed to both changes, and the school's ownership was transferred in 1850.

For many years, the transfer of ownership did not affect how the school was run. The school continued to teach religious classes and prepare some students for the ministry. Then the school started changing. It stopped teaching religion and became primarily an agricultural school. At that point, the Board of Missions claimed the government had violated the conditions and asked for the $15,000 it had agreed to pay.

Hawaii was a U.S. territory by this time, and the territorial court held that the Hawaiian government had not violated the agreement. The U.S. Supreme Court disagreed.

First, the Court ruled that the courts could look beyond the actual language in the agreement for other evidence of the parties' intent. Then it looked at the correspondence between the Board and the government of Hawaii when the transfer was made and determined that both parties understood that the school was to continue teaching the same religious doctrine. It held that "The provision for religious teaching is unchanging. It is as definite and absolute today as it was when it was written. The alternative of it the agreement has made the return of the property conveyed, or the payment of $15,000."[19] The Court said that the agreement required Hawaii to return the property or pay $15,000, and it sent the case back to the territorial court for action consistent with its holding.

The Hawaiian court did not like the Supreme Court's decision, so it keyed in on the Court's statement that the courts could look beyond the language of the agreement. The territorial court then looked at additional evidence and decided that the new evidence was stronger than the evidence the Supreme Court had reviewed. The territorial court then held—for a second time—that the parties had not intended to require the government to continue teaching religion and the government did not have to forfeit either the school or the $15,000.

The case reached the Supreme Court again, and the second opinion had no kind words for the territorial court. The Court said it had already determined what the parties intended, and the lower court should not have reopened the issue. But to make its point even stronger, it reviewed the additional evidence and found that it supported the Court's original conclusion: The parties agreed the school would continue teaching religious subjects. This time it left the territorial court no room to disagree. The Court directed it to enter judgment for the Board, meaning that the government was required to either return the school to the Board or pay $15,000.

Meyer v. Nebraska (1923)[20]
Ten-year-old Raymond Parpart was learning German at Zion Parochial School. His teacher, Mr. Meyer, used Bible stories to teach the language of their Lutheran heritage.

Unfortunately, Nebraska did not like what Mr. Meyer was doing. The state had passed a law prohibiting teaching foreign languages (except Latin and other "dead languages") in schools below high school. So the state arrested Mr. Meyer.

Although the Court used the Fourteenth Amendment to decide the case, it did not even mention the First Amendment. Instead, it used the Fourteenth Amendment's guarantee against depriving any person of liberty without due process of law. The Court recognized Nebraska's desire, in light of the recent war against Germany, to create unity by having all citizens speak the same language. It also recognized the state's right to prescribe a curriculum and to require those courses to be taught in English. But Nebraska's statute did more.

According to Justice McReynolds, the Nebraska statute arbitrarily interfered with "the calling of modern language teachers, with the opportunities of pupils to acquire knowledge, and with the power of parents to control the education of their own."[21] According to the Court, "No emergency has arisen which renders knowledge by a child of some language other than English so clearly harmful as to justify its inhibition, with the consequent infringement of rights long enjoyed."[22] The statute violated the Fourteenth Amendment's liberty guarantee, and Mr. Meyer was free to teach German to Raymond and any other student in his classroom.

Pierce v. Society of the Sisters of the Holy Names of Jesus and Mary (1925)[23]

The Society of Sisters had been operating Roman Catholic schools in Oregon for many years. In addition to religious training, the Catholic schools taught the same secular subjects as the public schools. Then the state passed a law requiring parents to send children between eight and sixteen to public schools. The Society objected to the new law, which it claimed deprived parents of the right to choose their children's schools.

The Supreme Court agreed. As in *Meyer*, it decided the case based on the liberty guaranteed by the Fourteenth Amendment rather than on the First Amendment. The Court reiterated that states have a valid interest in setting curriculum and ensuring that children receive an adequate education. But it held that there are limits to what a state can require. Justice McReynolds, again writing for the Court, said that the law "unreasonably interferes with the liberty of parents and guardians to direct the upbringing and education of children under their control. As often heretofore pointed out, rights guaranteed by the Constitution may not be abridged by legislation which has no reasonable relation to some purpose within the competency of the state."[24]

Cochran v. Louisiana State Board of Education (1930)[25]

Louisiana taxpayers challenged the state's right to spend tax money on textbooks that it then lent to all school children in the state for free. The taxpayers claimed that the payments to school children attending private schools were unconstitutional under the Fourteenth Amendment's prohibition on taking private public property for a private purpose because the state was taking private property (money paid as taxes) and using it for a private purpose.

The Court found that the funds were used for a public purpose: education. Chief Justice Hughes said, "We cannot doubt that the taxing power of the state is exerted for a public purpose. The legislation does not segregate private schools, or their pupils, as its beneficiaries, or attempt to interfere with any matters of exclusively private concern. Its interest is education, broadly; its method, comprehensive. Individual interests are aided only as the common interest is safeguarded."[26] Therefore, the state's use of the tax was valid, and it could lend textbooks to children attending private schools.

In this case the Court did not consider whether the payments violated the Establishment Clause because no one claimed that they did. As discussed in the next chapter, that would soon change.

Miscellaneous

During these silent periods the Court also decided a number of cases that do not fall into a particular category. Here are some of the more interesting ones.

Permoli v. New Orleans (1845)[27]

In 1842, New Orleans passed an ordinance prohibiting anyone from taking a corpse into any Roman Catholic Church except the obituary chapel. The ordinance did not apply to Protestants, who normally held their funerals at graveside.[28]

Father Permoli violated the ordinance by conducting a funeral service in a parish church. He was found guilty and fined $50. Then he appealed the case to the Supreme Court, claiming that the ordinance violated his religious liberty.

Unfortunately for Father Permoli, Louisiana was a state rather than a federal territory governed by Congress, the First Amendment only refers to actions by Congress, and the Fourteenth Amendment—which would eventually be used to apply the First Amendment to the states—had not even been thought of. The Court dismissed the case for lack of jurisdiction, noting that:

> The Constitution makes no provision for protecting the citizens of the respective states in their religious liberties; this is left to the state constitutions and laws: nor is there any inhibition imposed by the Constitution of the United States in this respect on the states.[29]

Hallett v. Collins (1850)[30]

Joseph Collins and Elizabeth Wilson were married in a civil ceremony in Louisiana in 1805, two years after the Louisiana Purchase and seven years before it became a state. Since the ceremony was not performed by a priest, many people did not accept the marriage as valid. So were their three sons legitimate?

The case before the Court involved a scheme to defraud Joseph's three sons of a piece of valuable land after he died. But first the only son still alive had to prove that Joseph's sons were his heirs. There was no question that Joseph and Elizabeth were their biological parents. In those days, however, a child could not inherit if he was illegitimate, so the Court had to decide whether the marriage was valid under the law that governed the Louisiana territory in 1805.

The question was complicated because Louisiana had belonged to two other countries (Spain and France) before the United States bought it, and both of those countries had adopted proclamations that were issued by the Council of Trent in 1563. One of those proclamations said that a marriage was not valid unless performed by a priest.

The Council of Trent was an ecclesiastical body, not a civil government, and the Court recognized that an ecclesiastical body could not affect someone's civil status. Still, civil governments can follow a church body's lead and adopt its rules, and most European countries did. So the Court reviewed a tangled web and traced Louisiana's laws back several centuries before concluding that the Council of Trent's marriage proclamation had never become part of Louisiana's civil law. So Joseph and Elizabeth were legally married and Sidney was legitimate. The Court also found that Sidney had been swindled out of the land and gave it back to him.

Cummings v. Missouri (1866)[31]

The Reverend Mr. Cummings, a Roman Catholic priest, was convicted of teaching and preaching in Missouri without taking a loyalty oath. He was fined $500 and sent to prison until he paid the fine.

The Missouri law he violated was adopted at the end of the Civil War. It prohibited anyone from holding public office or practicing certain professions—including that of priest or clergyman—unless he took an oath affirming that he had not fought for the Confederacy, given support or aid to any person fighting for the Confederacy, or left the state to avoid being drafted by the Union army.[32]

Rev. Cummings argued that the oath violated Article I, Section 10 of the U.S. Constitution, which prohibits states from passing bills of attainder (laws that inflict punishment without a trial) and *ex post facto* laws (laws that punish people for behavior that was not illegal at the time).[33] Missouri argued that the law did not violate the Constitution because it merely punished current behavior—failure to take the oath—and that failure had been the subject of a trial.

Recognizing that the First Amendment did not apply to the states, Rev. Cummings did not argue that the oath violated his freedom of religion. Still, his attorney referred to the principles behind the Free Exercise Clause and framed the issue this way:

> The issue is whether the Church shall be free or not to exercise her natural and inherent right of calling into, or rejecting from, her ministry whom she pleases; whether yielding to the dictation of the civil power she shall admit those only who, according to its judgment, are fit for office, or, admitting those to be fit, whether she shall not be free to admit those also who, though at first not fit, afterwards become so through pardon and forgiveness.[34]

Five justices agreed with Rev. Cummings. The Court found that the oath violated Article I because it punished past conduct—siding with or rendering support to persons who sided with the Confederacy—without a trial by taking away the right to practice certain professions unless the person took the oath. Although the justices recognized that the vocation at issue in this case was that of priest or clergyman, the Court did not make any distinction between it and nonreligious professions, such as practicing law.

Church of the Holy Trinity v. United States (1892)[35]

Holy Trinity Church in New York City wanted to call Rev. Walpole Warren to be its pastor. Rev. Warren was from England, so he moved to New York after the church sent him a contract. Then the U.S. government stepped in and claimed that the contract violated a law that prohibited bringing in workers from another country.

The Supreme Court conceded that Holy Trinity Church's arrangement with Rev. Warren was prohibited by the letter of the law, which was broadly written with no exception for ministers or other professionals. But the justices were reluctant to apply it to this case. Instead, they looked at the law's legislative history and determined that Congress adopted the law because employers were bringing unskilled workers to the United States who would work for lower wages than the surplus of unskilled workers already in this country. The Court concluded that Congress did not intend the law to cover "brain toilers" such as ministers. Therefore, it held that the law did not apply to Holy Trinity Church and Rev. Warren.

That was all the Court needed to say to decide the case. But Justice Brewer went further. His opinion for the Court stated that "no purpose of action against religion can be imputed to any legislation, state or national, because this is a religious people."[36] Justice Brewer also included another statement and a question. "[T]his is a Christian nation. In the face of all these, shall it be believed that a Congress of the United States intended to make it a misdemeanor for a church of this country to contract for the services of a Christian minister residing in another nation?"[37] And he answered the question in the negative.

Bradfield v. Roberts (1899)[38]

The District of Columbia entered into a contract with Providence Hospital, which was run by a Catholic religious order. Under the contract, the United States Government would pay for a new hospital wing, and the hospital would use the wing to provide medical services to poor residents of Washington, D.C., Bradfield did not want his taxes spent that way, so he sued the U.S. Treasurer to keep the government from financing the new wing.

Bradfield argued that the contract violated the Establishment Clause because it required Congress to pay money to a religious society. The Court ignored the Establishment Clause, however. Although a religious order ran it, the hospital was a separate corporation formed for a single purpose: to provide medical care. The Court decided that the hospital was not a religious institution, and the contract was good.[39]

Hygrade Provision Co. v. Sherman (1925)[40]

Although most of the early religion cases involved Christians, a New York case involved Jews. New York City adopted an ordinance prohibiting people from selling meat they falsely claimed was kosher. Several businesses challenged the ordinance, claiming that it put them at risk of violating it unintentionally because the meaning of "kosher" was unclear.

The Supreme Court rejected their argument. First, it found that the word "kosher" had an established meaning among the Jewish community, so the ordinance was not unclear. It also noted that the statute only prohibited fraudulent behavior; honest mistakes were not covered. And the city had the right to protect its citizens from misleading advertising. So the ordinance was valid.

As already noted, the First Amendment says that "*Congress* shall make no law," and *Permoli* specifically recognized that the Constitution did not prohibit the states from interfering with their citizens' religious freedom. The Fourteenth Amendment—which does apply to the states—was ratified in 1868 but did not mention religion. It was not until the late 1930s that the Court started using the Fourteenth Amendment to apply the First Amendment's Religion Clauses to the states.

Question 1: In *Rector of Holy Trinity Church v. United States,* Justice Brewer stated that America is a Christian Nation. What makes a country a Christian Nation? And how much do the Supreme Court's decisions have to do with it?

Question 2: Many of the early religion cases were property or inheritance disputes. Why do you think there were so few cases involving religious conduct?

CHAPTER SIX
FROM CLASSROOM
TO COURTROOM

Seventh grade. Low self-esteem. A search for identity. Peer pressure and a desire to belong. This is the stage of life that Donna Schempp was in when the State of Pennsylvania required public schools to start the day with oral Bible readings—readings that conflicted with Donna's Unitarian faith.

Donna did not complain to her teachers or the school administration. In fact, she even volunteered to be one of the readers. All she wanted was to fit in.

Donna's older brother Ellory was more self-assured. As a high school junior, he protested by reading a copy of the Koran to himself while the Bible was being read and by refusing to stand during the Lord's Prayer. Ellory's teacher sent him to the vice principal's office to discuss the matter, and he spent the rest of the year in the guidance counselor's office during morning devotions. The next year the assistant principal told Ellory to stay in the room during the Bible reading, and he did.[1]

onna Schempp's case is just one of many Establishment Clause cases decided by the U.S. Supreme Court. This chapter looks at cases involving schools. The next chapter will explore the Establishment Clause cases involving public religious displays and the potpourri of cases that do not fit neatly elsewhere.

The Early Landmark Cases
The 1947 case of *Everson v. Board of Education* was the first case to explore the Establishment Clause in depth.[2] A New Jersey statute authorized local school districts to pay for children's transportation to and from school, and the Ewing Township Board of Education voted to reimburse parents for travel costs to and from both public and not-for-profit private (mostly Catholic) schools.

Everson objected to having his taxes pay for transportation to parochial school. So he sued the Board, claiming that the payments violated the Establishment Clause. Five members of the Supreme Court disagreed with Everson and held that the statute, and the school board's action under it, was constitutional. According to the Court, all it did was "provide a general program to help parents get their children, regardless of their religion, safely and expeditiously to and from accredited schools."[3]

Even though the majority upheld the school board's action, Justice Black's opinion for the Court endorsed the separation of church and state. He described the Establishment Clause as follows:

> The "establishment of religion" clause of the First Amendment means at least this: Neither a state nor the Federal Government can set up a church. Neither can pass laws which aid one religion, aid all religions, or prefer one religion over another. Neither can force nor influence a person to go or to remain away from church against his will or force him to profess a belief or disbelief in any religion. No person can be punished for entertaining or professing religious beliefs or disbeliefs, for church attendance or non-attendance. No tax in any amount, large or small, can be levied to support any religious activities or institutions, whatever they may be called, or whatever form they may adopt to teach or practice religion. Neither a state nor the Federal Government can, openly or secretly, participate in the affairs of any religious organizations or groups and *vice versa*. In the words of Jefferson, the clause against establishment of religion by law was intended to erect "a wall of separation between Church and State."[4]

Four Justices dissented. Justice Rutledge's dissent reviewed the legislative history behind the Establishment Clause and concluded that the people who adopted it intended "to create a complete and permanent separation of the spheres of religious activity and civil authority by comprehensively forbidding every form of public aid or support for religion."[5]

Both Justice Black's opinion and Justice Rutledge's dissent are frequently cited in the battle over the meaning of the Establishment Clause. Both looked at the framers' intent, primarily based on the indirect legislative history discussed in Chapter 4 of this book. And both concluded that the First Amendment had erected an impregnable wall between church and state. Their only disagreement was on what breached the wall; Black said that payments to all students for transportation costs did not, and Justice Rutledge said they did.

Everson did not develop a test the Court could use in later cases. That test came twenty-four years later in *Lemon v. Kurtzman.*[6]

Lemon and its companion cases challenged Pennsylvania and Rhode Island statutes that authorized salary supplements for teachers who taught secular subjects in private schools, most of which were parochial schools. The Pennsylvania statute reimbursed schools for certain educational expenses, including teachers' salaries, textbooks, and instructional materials for secular classes. The state could not, however, pay expenses for courses that included any religious content.

The Rhode Island statute paid a 15-percent salary supplement to teachers employed by schools with below-average expenditures per student. To qualify, the teacher had to teach secular courses only, use materials that the public schools used, and agree not to teach religion classes.

In holding both statutes unconstitutional, Chief Justice Burger articulated a three-prong test. Under *Lemon*, a case must meet each prong to survive an Establishment Clause challenge:

- The statute must have a secular legislative purpose (the purpose test),
- Its principal effect must neither advance nor inhibit religion, although religion can benefit indirectly (the effect test), and
- It must not excessively entangle government with religion (the entanglement test).

The *Lemon* test was later modified by *Agostini v. Felton.*[7] *Agostini* said that the degree of entanglement between government and religion is just one factor to consider under the effect test, eliminating it as a separate basis for finding that government action violates the Establishment Clause.

Since *Everson*, the Supreme Court has considered a number of cases involving religious activities in public schools. They include prayer, the evolution versus creationism debate, church-sponsored religious activities held during the school day or on school property; and government aid to religious schools.

Prayer, Bible Reading, and the Ten Commandments

Some of the most emotional and divisive public school cases involve religious activities that are affirmatively sponsored or endorsed by the state or the school district. These cases cover prayer, Bible reading, and displaying the Ten Commandments.

Engel v. Vitale (1962)[8]

The New York Board of Regents recommended that all local school districts start the school day with a prayer to "Almighty God." State officials composed the prayer, which they included in a "Statement on Moral and Spiritual Training in the Schools." The Statement said it would be "subscribed to by all men and women of good will"—implying that anyone who disagreed was acting from bad motives.[9] Union Free School District No. 9 of Hyde Park adopted the prayer and directed students to say it aloud at the beginning of each school day. A group of parents objected to the practice and took their constitutional challenge all the way to the U.S. Supreme Court.

The Court held that requiring public school students to say a state-sponsored prayer violates the Establishment Clause. Although the Court had not yet articulated the *Lemon* purpose test, it was clear that the Board of Regents had a religious purpose in composing the prayer and recommending its use, and that motive probably factored into the Court's decision.

The lower courts had upheld using the prayer on the condition that the schools excused students from participating if their parents objected. But the "voluntary" nature of the prayer did not save it. As Justice Black stated in his opinion for the Court:

> The Establishment Clause, unlike the Free Exercise Clause, does not depend upon any showing of direct governmental compulsion and is violated by the enactment of laws which establish an official religion whether those laws operate directly to coerce nonobserving individuals or not. This is not to say, of course, that laws officially prescribing a particular form of religious worship do not involve coercion of such individuals. When the power, prestige and financial support of a government is placed behind a particular religious belief, the indirect coercive pressure upon religious minorities to conform to the prevailing officially approved religion is plain.[10]

School District of Abington Township v. Schempp (1963)[11]

While *Engel* was making its way through the courts, Donna Schempp's parents filed a lawsuit challenging a Pennsylvania law, and Madalyn Murray (later Madalyn Murray O'Hare) filed a lawsuit challenging a similar law in Maryland. The Pennsylvania law required that public schools start their day with a Bible reading, without comment, of at least ten verses. It also allowed parents to send a note to school asking that their children be excused from class during the daily exercises. But Donna was twelve years old, and what 12-year-old girl wants to be singled out in that way? And, even though the school administration knew that Donna's older brother Ellory objected to the exercises, it encouraged him to stay in class his senior year. In the Schempps' case, voluntary did not mean willing.

As in *Engel*, the activity challenged by Schempp and Murray clearly had a religious purpose. This was the Court's principal reason for condemning it. According to the Court:

> The test may be stated as follows: what are the purpose and the primary effect of the enactment? If either is the advancement or inhibition of religion then the enactment exceeds the scope of legislative power as circumscribed by the Constitution. That is to

say that to withstand the strictures of the Establishment Clause there must be a secular legislative purpose and a primary effect that neither advances nor inhibits religion.[12]

Wallace v. Jaffree (1985)[13]

The purpose of the legislation also determined the outcome in *Wallace v. Jaffree.* In that case the Supreme Court struck down an Alabama statute authorizing a period of silence in the public schools "for meditation or voluntary prayer."

Ishmael Jaffree was a resident of Mobile County, Alabama, with two children in second grade and one in kindergarten. He complained that his children's teachers led their classes in daily unison prayers, that the children were ostracized by their classmates if they did not participate, and that he had repeatedly but unsuccessfully asked that the prayers be eliminated.

The legislator who had sponsored the bill in the state senate admitted that his sole motive was to return voluntary prayer to the public schools. The Court also noted that an existing statute already protected a student's right to engage in silent prayer, and the "meditation" statute did not serve any secular purpose that was not already being met.

Lee v. Weisman (1992)[14]

Deborah Weisman graduated from middle school in 1989. Her father knew that the school system always invited a minister, priest, or rabbi to give an invocation and benediction at each middle school and high school graduation ceremony, so he objected in advance to having prayers at Deborah's graduation. But the school system did not honor his objection. Rather than missing an important milestone in her life, Deborah and her family attended the graduation and sat through the prayers.

The Court held that the practice of including prayers as part of the official public school graduation ceremony violated the Establishment Clause. The Court recognized that subtle coercion can be especially effective in some situations, noting that few high school seniors will choose to skip their graduation ceremonies in order to avoid sitting through prayers that are contrary to their beliefs.

Santa Fe Independent School Dist. v. Doe (2000)[15]
Until 1995, Santa Fe High School students annually elected an official student council chaplain, and one of the chaplain's duties was to pray over the public address system before each varsity football game. After a lawsuit was filed, the school district adopted a different policy that permitted, but did not require, students to initiate and lead prayers at all home games. This policy provided for a two-step process. The students would first vote to decide if they wanted a prayer. If that passed, a second vote would be held to select a particular student to deliver it.

On August 31, 1995, the students voted to start each football game with a student-led prayer, and a week later they held another election to select someone to say it. Still facing court action, the policy was again changed in October to eliminate the word "prayer" and replace it with "messages," "statements," and "invocations." No other changes were made.

This case was brought by two families—one Mormon and one Catholic—who did not want to be identified because they did not want their children to be ostracized. The district court judge let them file and prosecute it anonymously.

The Supreme Court ruled that the Establishment Clause prevented school districts from requiring high school students to choose between attending school football games and staying true to their religious beliefs. It held that prayers given by students at official school events—in this case varsity football games—violate the Establishment Clause if the school sets the rules, provides the facilities, and oversees the activity.[16]

... one of the purposes of the Bill of Rights is to protect the minority against the tyranny of the majority, and allowing the majority to take away rights guaranteed by the Constitution is not acceptable.

The Court also explained that Establishment Clause rights do not depend on the desires of the majority. The school policy allowed the student body to vote on whether to have prayer before the football games. But one of the purposes of the Bill of Rights is to protect the minority against the tyranny of the majority, and allowing the majority to take away rights guaranteed by the Constitution is not acceptable.

Stone v. Graham (1980)_[17]
In *Stone v. Graham,* a Kentucky statute also failed the purpose test.[18] The statute required all public schools to post a copy of the Ten Commandments, purchased with private funds, on the wall of each classroom. The Court held that the statute had no secular legislative purpose. The opinion went on to state:

> This is not a case in which the Ten Commandments are integrated into the school curriculum, where the Bible may constitutionally be used in an appropriate study of history, civilization, ethics, comparative religion, or the like. Posting of religious texts on the wall serves no such educational function.

The Court did not say the Ten Commandments must be banned from the public schools. But it did say they could not be used for religious reasons.

Although the Supreme Court may have taken state-sponsored prayer out of the public schools, it has never interfered with a Christian's right to pray privately in school or anywhere else. As Justice Stevens, writing for the *Doe* Court, stated:

> [N]othing in the Constitution as interpreted by this Court prohibits any public school student from voluntarily praying at any time before, during, or after the school day. But the religious liberty protected by the Constitution is abridged when the State affirmatively sponsors the particular religious practice of prayer.[19]

Evolution
The prayer and Bible-reading cases invalidated governmental actions that supported a belief in God, but the evolution cases were even more specific. These did not just support a belief in God or the Christian religion; they defended a particular Christian ideology.

Epperson v. Arkansas (1968)[20]
Susan Epperson taught biology in a public high school in Little Rock, Arkansas. An Arkansas statute made it illegal to teach evolution in any public school or state university, and until 1965 the biology textbook endorsed by the school did not include information on evolution. But then the school administration acted on the advice of the biology teachers in the school system and adopted a new textbook that did.

If Susan taught the chapter on evolution, she would commit a crime and could get fired. If she did not, she would be ignoring an entire section of the new textbook. And it appears from the record that she did not want to ignore it. So what did she do? She sued.

The Court unanimously voted to strike down the Arkansas statute, although they did not all agree on the reason. But seven Justices held that the Establishment Clause "does not permit the State to require that teaching and learning must be tailored to the principles or prohibitions of any religious sect or dogma."[21] Justice Fortas, speaking for the Court, went on to note that Arkansas was attempting to do just that.

> "In the present case, there can be no doubt that Arkansas has sought to prevent its teachers from discussing the theory of evolution because it is contrary to the belief of some that the Book of Genesis must be the exclusive source of doctrine as to the origin of man. No suggestion has been made that Arkansas' law may be justified by considerations of state policy other than the religious views of some of its citizens."[22]

As a result of the Court's ruling, Arkansas could not prohibit its public school teachers from teaching evolution. The opinion suggested, however, that a more even-handed approach might be constitutional.

Edwards v. Aguillard (1987)[23]
Louisiana took that suggestion to heart and adopted a law that required any teacher who taught evolution to also teach creation science. Then a group of parents, teachers, and religious leaders challenged it.

The Supreme Court held the Louisiana statute unconstitutional. According to the Court, "the purpose of the Creationism Act was to restructure the science curriculum to conform to a particular religious viewpoint. Out of many possible science subjects taught in the public schools, the legislature chose to affect the teaching of the one scientific theory that historically has been opposed by certain religious sects."[24]

Louisiana said it adopted the statute to protect academic freedom, but the statute actually hurt academic freedom by reducing teachers' options from four (teach both, teach evolution only, teach creationism only, or teach neither) to two (teach both or teach neither). The Court found that Louisiana's stated purpose was a sham and that the law's real purpose was to promote a particular religious theory (creationism), or at least to minimize the harm to that theory by counterbalancing the effect of teaching evolution. Because the statute was designed to protect a particular religious view, it violated the Establishment Clause.

Released Time

Can public schools release students during the school day to attend religious instruction? The Court heard two cases in less than five years and reached different conclusions based on their facts.

In *McCollum v. Board of Education* (1948), the Champaign, Illinois, school district allowed a coalition of Jewish, Catholic, and Protestant groups to come onto school premises during the school day and provide religious education to those children whose parents had consented.[25] The religious classes were held in the classrooms, and the students whose parents had not consented were sent elsewhere in the building to study.

According to the Supreme Court, school authorities had sponsored the religious activities in three ways: by using the compulsory attendance laws to give the coalition a captive audience, by allowing the classes to be conducted on school grounds, and by allowing them to be conducted during school hours. Therefore, the Court found the practice unconstitutional under the Establishment Clause.

A few years later, the Court decided *Zorach v. Clauson* (1952) and reached a different conclusion.[26] The only significant difference between *Zorach* and *McCollum* was the location of the religious instruction. In *Zorach* the classes were held off school premises although they were still held during the school day.[27] *Zorach* did not overrule *McCollum*, however, and it is difficult to tell how the Court would handle these same facts today.

Except for *Zorach*, none of these religious activity cases got beyond the purpose test. But even if they had, the results would probably not have changed since they all preferred some religious beliefs over others. In *Engel* and the other prayer cases, the state or the school districts gave preferred status to religions that believe in a Supreme Being (as opposed to religions that believe in a number of gods or to atheism). In *Stone* and *McCollum*, the legislators or school officials gave preferred status to the Judeo-Christian religions. The law in *Schempp* gave preferred status to Christianity, and the evolution statutes gave preferred status to Christians with a particular belief about how the world was created.

Government Aid to Religious Schools

Purpose is not an issue in most of the school aid cases. The Court recognizes the government has a valid secular purpose to see that every child within its boundaries gets a quality education. The outcome of the school aid cases tends to depend instead on the second prong of *Lemon*: the effect test. Here are some of the more significant ones.

Everson v. Board of Education of Ewing Township (1947)[28]
The facts in the *Everson* school bus case were not as developed as in later cases, but the information in the Court's opinion shows that the payments probably would have met both the purpose and the effect test. First, the majority assumed that the New Jersey legislature had a public purpose for reimburs-

ing transportation expenses, and the fact that public school students also received free transportation supported that assumption.

As for the effect test, several facts supported the conclusion that the law's principal effect did not advance religion. First, the payments went to the parents, not to the parochial school. Second, transportation cannot impart doctrine, so even if the students themselves were impressionable, the activity the funds supported could not sway them one way or the other. Third, the reimbursements were available to parents of public school students as well as parents of parochial school students. All of these considerations support *Everson*'s ultimate conclusion: Reimbursing parents for the cost of public transportation to parochial schools does not, by itself, violate the Establishment Clause.

Board of Education v. Allen (1968)[29]

A New York law required local school boards to lend textbooks free of charge to all students in seventh through twelfth grade. The textbooks were available to all students within the state on the same terms; the school board lent the textbooks directly to the students, not to the schools; and they were available to any student who requested them without regard to the type of school the student attended. And only textbooks approved for use in the public schools were eligible, making it unlikely that their contents would indoctrinate students to a religious viewpoint. Given these facts, the Court found that loaning textbooks to parochial school children did not violate the Establishment Clause.

Lemon v. Kurtzman (1971)[30]

Up to this point, all of the decisions upheld government support. Then the Court decided *Lemon*.

Pennsylvania and Rhode Island had adopted statutes authorizing salary supplements for teachers who taught secular subjects in private schools. Pennsylvania paid the supplements to the schools, and Rhode Island paid them to the teachers.

The Court formulated the now-famous *Lemon* test and applied it to the Pennsylvania and Rhode Island statutes. Both statutes had a secular purpose—to attract qualified teachers and ensure the quality of the secular education in all schools covered by the compulsory attendance laws—so they passed the purpose test before they ran into trouble.

Most of the teachers that benefited from the supplements taught in Catholic schools, so the Court discussed the nature of those schools. The Court concluded that parochial schools were an integral part of the Catholic Church's mission and had a great deal of influence in forming students' religious beliefs, especially during the more impressionable elementary school years. It also concluded that the teachers who received the salary supplements might let their religious beliefs color the way they taught their secular subjects.

> We need not and do not assume that teachers in parochial schools will be guilty of bad faith or any conscious design to evade the limitations imposed by the statute and the First Amendment. We simply recognize that a dedicated religious person, teaching in a school affiliated with his or her faith and operated to inculcate its tenets, will inevitably experience great difficulty in remaining religiously neutral.[31]

Both Pennsylvania and Rhode Island had adopted administrative requirements designed to ensure that the funds were not used for religious purposes. For example, the Pennsylvania statute required the schools to keep extensive records of their expenditures and to allow the state to audit those records. These requirements were necessary to ensure that the salary supplements met the effect test. Yet they also ensured that it failed the entanglement test.

Witters v. Washington Department of Services for the Blind (1986)[32]
Larry Witters was attending Inland Empire School of the Bible to become a pastor, missionary, or youth director. He was also going blind, and he qualified for state assistance because of his condition. When Larry filed an assistance application with the Washington Commission for the Blind, however, they denied it because he was pursuing a degree in theology.

The Washington State Supreme Court affirmed the denial, ruling that the Establishment Clause of the First Amendment prohibited paying assistance for theological degrees. The U.S. Supreme Court reversed, noting that the Commission would send the money to Larry, not to the Inland Empire School, and he could use it any way he wanted. Using it to attend a Christian school was his choice, not the state's. Therefore, the payments would not violate the Establishment Clause.

The case did not end there, however. It went back to the Washington State Supreme Court, which then ruled that state assistance that helps someone get a theological education violated the state constitution. So Larry did not get the aid.[33]

Zobrest v. Catalina Foothills School District (1993)[34]
James Zobrest had been deaf since birth. He went to a school for the deaf through fifth grade, and he then attended a public middle school. While he was in middle school, the school district provided a sign language interpreter to accompany him to school and interpret his classes. When he decided to go to a Catholic high school, he wanted the public school board to continue paying for a sign language interpreter. But the school board claimed that would violate the Establishment Clause.

The Court did not agree. It noted that a sign language interpreter would merely pass on information that James received from others—the teachers—and would not add his or her own religious spin to the information being interpreted. It also noted that it was James's parents choice to send him to a Catholic school, not the state's choice to subsidize a private school. Then the Court held that the Establishment Clause does not prevent a school district from providing a sign language interpreter even though the interpreter would be interpreting religious as well as secular lectures.

Agostini v. Felton (1997)[35]
Can New York City provide remedial education to disadvantaged children who attend parochial schools with violating the Establishment Clause? In 1997, the Court said "yes."

As noted above, the Court also eliminated entanglement as a separate test. *Agostini* set out three primary criteria that the Court's more recent cases use in deciding whether government aid to parochial schools meets the effect test. Each criterion asks a question.

- Is the form of the aid free from religious indoctrination?
- Is the aid available to everyone without creating an incentive for parents to send their children to religious schools?
- Does it avoid excessively entangling government in the religious institution's affairs?

If all three answers are "yes," the aid does not advance or inhibit religion.

Mitchell v. Helms (2000)[36]

The 2000 case of *Mitchell v. Helms* further refined the religious indoctrination test. Jefferson Parish, Louisiana, lent educational materials and equipment to both public and private schools. According to Justice Thomas's plurality opinion, any aid suitable for use in a public school passes the test. Even aid that can be diverted to a religious use may pass the test if the only reason it can be diverted is because the parents have made an independent private choice to send their children to a parochial school.

As discussed in Chapter 2, in rare cases the Supreme Court will decide that an earlier decision is no longer consistent with its more recent decisions and will overrule it. The Court did just that in *Agostini v. Felton,* in which it overruled earlier cases holding that remedial services provided by public school employees to parochial school students on parochial school premises violated the Establishment Clause, and in *Mitchell v. Helms,* in which it overruled earlier cases holding that the loan of educational materials and equipment (e.g., maps and projectors) to private schools violated the Establishment Clause.[37]

Since *Everson*, the Supreme Court has considered a number of cases involving government support to parochial elementary and secondary schools. In almost every case, the Court has recognized a primary secular purpose: to provide a quality education to all students within the governmental unit's geographical boundaries.

In a string of cases from the 1970s that are still in effect today, the Court found that the following types of support violated the Establishment Clause:

- Salary supplements to private school teachers (1971)[38]
- Expenses (including salary expenses) incurred by private schools in connection with administering and grading teacher-created tests (1973)[39]
- Direct money grants for maintaining and repairing school buildings where the grants are not limited to secular facilities (meaning that the funds could be used to maintain and repair the school chapel) (1973)[40]
- Tuition reimbursement available only to parents of private school students [41]
- Educational tax deductions or credits available only to parents of private school students (1973) [42]

In each case, the aid was either susceptible to an ideological use (for example, a science teacher might teach creation from a Biblical point of view and create tests that favor that point of view) or was available only to private schools or private school parents.

These cases are just one side of the coin, however. The Supreme Court has validated most forms of non-ideological aid available to all schools, both public and private, or to all parents. Applying these principles, the Court has upheld support in the form of:

- Reimbursement for bus transportation to and from school (1947)[43]

- Textbook loans (1968)[44]
- Expenses (including salary expenses) to administer standardized tests and to grade multiple-choice and other standardized test questions that have only one right answer (1980)[45]
- Expenses (including salary expenses) for state-required recordkeeping and reporting (e.g., statistical information, attendance records) (1980)[46]
- Income tax deductions for educational expenses available to all parents regardless of where their children attend school, even if tuition is one of the deductible expenses (1983)[47]
- Sign language interpreters available to all deaf students attending public or private schools, even though the interpreter will interpret religious as well as secular classes (1993)[48]
- Remedial education in secular subjects provided to all students, public and private, even if provided on parochial school premises (1997)[49]
- Loans of secular educational materials and equipment that are also provided to public schools (2000)[50]
- Tuition vouchers available to all low-income parents to provide them with educational choices, where the overall effect of the program provides incentives to attend public schools that are equal to or greater than those to attend private schools (2002)[51]

Even before *Agostini* and *Mitchell*, the Court was more likely to uphold governmental aid as the students became less susceptible to religious influence. In one line of cases, the Supreme Court upheld governmental aid to Christian colleges to fund buildings and facilities used for secular purposes.[52] As Chief Justice Burger said in *Tilton v. Richardson*:

> There are generally significant differences between the religious aspects of church-related institutions of higher learning and parochial elementary and secondary schools. The "affirmative if not dominant policy" of the instruction in pre-college church

schools is "to assure future adherents to a particular faith by having control of their total education at an early age." There is substance to the contention that college students are less impressionable and less susceptible to religious indoctrination. Common observation would seem to support that view, and Congress may well have entertained it. The skepticism of the college student is not an inconsiderable barrier to any attempt or tendency to subvert the congressional objectives and limitations.[53]

One of the most interesting Supreme Court cases is *Board of Education of Kiryas Joel Village School District v. Grumet.*[54] In that 1994 case, the Supreme Court struck down a law specifically designed to favor a religious group. Everyone who lived in Kiryas Joel was a Satmar Hasidim Jew. This religious group spoke Yiddish as its primary language and made few concessions to the modern world. The village was part of a larger public school district, but all of the children from the village went to private schools run by the Satmar Hasidim Jews. There was only one problem—the private schools did not offer special services for handicapped children. The law required public school districts to provide those services, and the local school district attempted to accommodate the village children without violating the Establishment Clause as interpreted by the Court at that time (in cases that have since been overruled). For various reasons, however, its efforts failed. The New York legislature then passed a special law creating a new school district with the same boundaries as the village.

The Supreme Court's biggest concern was that the law was not one of general application. As Justice Souter noted in his opinion for the Court, "Because the religious community of Kiryas Joel did not receive its new governmental authority simply as one of many communities eligible for equal treatment under a general law, we have no assurance that the next similarly situated group seeking a school district of its own will receive one; . . ."[55] It was also obvious that the purpose of the special law was to benefit a particular religious group. Although the legislature's motive was secular—to provide a more effective means for delivering educational services to the disabled children in the village—it was obvious that the purpose and effect of the special law was to benefit a particular religious group. Based on these facts, the Court held that the special law violated the Establishment Clause.

Decisions in cases decided after *Lemon* have characterized the *Lemon* test as guidance rather than a hard-and-fast rule. Even used as guidance, however, the *Lemon* test is too abstract to apply to individual cases. This is particularly true of the second prong: When does a statute's primary effect advance or inhibit religion?

Although the Court has not articulated a more concrete test, it bases its decisions on practical considerations that seek to apply the intent—if not the letter—of the *Lemon* test. The Court asks several questions:

- What is the government's motive? If it wants to benefit or inhibit a particular religion or religion in general, the legislation is unconstitutional. This is how the Court applies the purpose test. And it usually accepts the legislation's stated purpose at face value, applying its own judgment only if it is clear that the stated purpose is not the real one.
- Is the legislation evenhanded? In other words, does it apply across-the-board or does it only apply to religious groups? This neutrality principle is the most important factor in applying the effect test (whether a statute's principal effect advances or inhibits religion).
- Is a religious organization or entity a direct beneficiary of the legislation? If the answer is yes, the legislation is more likely to be unconstitutional. This is only one factor to consider in determining the statute's princi-

pal effect, however, and more recent cases have transformed it into a different question: Do the benefits to the religious organization flow from the independent private choices of parents or from incentives provided by the government?

- Is the audience impressionable? The younger the students, the more likely that the legislation is unconstitutional. But this is only one factor to consider in determining the statute's principal effect.
- How much must the government intrude on the religious organization to ensure that it is complying with the law? The more it intrudes, the more likely the Court is to declare the statute unconstitutional. Since *Agostini*, this is just another factor to consider when applying the effect test.

The significance of each factor varies with the type of case.

Except for several cases that have since been overruled, the Court commonly upholds aid to schools run by religious groups or to parents who send their children to those schools if the aid is secular in nature and is available to all schools—public or private—or to all parents. The Supreme Court's decisions do not uphold aid that singles out religious schools (or private schools in general) or parents of parochial school students or that has an ideological component.

Question 1: The Supreme Court's decisions take state-sponsored prayers out of the public schools but do not prevent students from praying on their own initiative. What practical effects do these cases have on Christianity? Does leaving the decision up the the child strengthen or weaken the child's faith?

Question 2: Review the first hypothetical case at the beginning of Chapter 1. Based on its past cases, is the Supreme Court likely to find that the Cane County School Board dress code banning religious jewelry is a violation of the Establishment Clause? Why or why not?

CHAPTER SEVEN
AWAY WITH THE MANGER

Thomas Van Orden had taken the same route for six years, walking through the grounds of the Texas State Capitol on his almost
daily trips to the law library. For a homeless lawyer suspended
from practicing law, the library had become his refuge. And the
walk might have been pleasant except for one thing—it took him
past a 6-foot-high monument of the Ten Commandments written
on stone tablets.[1]

Did the monument violate the Establishment Clause of the First
Amendment? Van Orden thought so. In 2002 he acted on his belief and sued state officials to have it removed. The District Court
and the Fifth Circuit Court of Appeals both denied Van Orden's
request. And so he became one of the privileged few to have their
cases reach the United States Supreme Court.

Van Orden v. Perry is one of the latest Supreme Court cases deciding how the Establishment Clause applies to
public religious displays. This chapter starts with those
cases, moves on to the significant Establishment Clause cases
dealing with employment and taxes, and concludes with those
cases that do not fit neatly into a particular category.

Public Religious Displays
When a public religious display is involved, the cases usually
look at its purpose and its context. If its purpose is to endorse
religion, or if a viewer is likely to believe that the government is
endorsing religion, then the display violates the Establishment
Clause. Otherwise, it does not.

Stone v. Graham (1980)[2]
A Kentucky statute required schools to post a copy of the Ten
Commandments on the wall of each public school classroom.

The copies were purchased with private funds, and the following statement appeared, in small print, at the bottom: "The secular application of the Ten Commandments is clearly seen in its adoption as the fundamental legal code of Western Civilization and the Common Law of the United States."

In a very brief decision, the Supreme Court held that the Kentucky statute had no secular legislative purpose—which, by default, means it had a religious purpose. As a result, the statute violated the Establishment Clause, and the public schools had to remove the copies from their classrooms.

Lynch v. Donnelly (1984)[3]

Pawtucket, Rhode Island, set up an annual Christmas display in a park owned by a nonprofit organization and located in the heart of the shopping district. The display included Santa Claus's house, Santa's sleigh pulled by reindeer, a Christmas tree, candy-striped poles, carolers, a large banner that said "Season's Greetings," and a Nativity scene. Although a private entity owned the park, the city owned the Nativity scene and the rest of the display.

The American Civil Liberties Union sued the city to remove the Nativity scene. It won in the District Court and the First Circuit Court of Appeals but lost in the Supreme Court. The Court found that Pawtucket sponsored the display to celebrate a national holiday and to show its origins, which the Court said were legitimate secular purposes. Therefore, the display did not violate the Establishment Clause and the Nativity scene could stay.

The opinion says very little about how or why the Court reached its conclusions. Still, the crèche was just one part of a large display containing a number of items that had no religious significance whatsoever. And, as the next religious display case shows, context is everything.

County of Allegheny v. ACLU (1989)[4]

Visitors to the Allegheny County Courthouse in downtown Pittsburgh saw a large crèche displayed prominently on the Grand

Staircase. The traditional figures included an angel with a banner proclaiming "Gloria in Excelsis Deo." A wooden fence surrounded the manger scene on three sides, and a sign attached to the fence stated that a Roman Catholic group donated the display. The county put red and white poinsettias and a couple of small evergreen trees around the display and used it as a backdrop for carolers who performed during lunchtime.

A block away, the city set up a display outside the entry doors to the City-County Building. The most noticeable part of the display was the 45-foot Christmas tree, decorated with lights and ornaments, which stood in front of the middle of three arched doorways. Next to it was an 18-foot Chanukah menorah owned by a Jewish group. The display also contained a sign labeling it "Salute to Liberty."

The ACLU sued both the city and the county. It objected to the crèche and the menorah, but it did not object to the Christmas tree—apparently conceding that the tree had taken on a secular meaning. A fractured Supreme Court held that the crèche violated the Establishment Clause but the menorah did not.

Four justices voted that both the manger scene and the menorah violated the Establishment Clause, and four justices voted that neither did. Justice Blackmun was the swing vote that split the decision.

Blackmun reached different conclusions based on the context of the two displays. He started his analysis by noting that Christmas and Chanukah have both religious and secular aspects and that the Establishment Clause does not prohibit government from recognizing and celebrating the secular aspects of those holidays. Then he analyzed the displays themselves.

According to Blackmun, the menorah is primarily a religious symbol but has gained some secular meaning in that many nonpracticing Jewish households use it when they celebrate Chanukah. The Christmas tree, on the other hand, has become a secular symbol of Christmas. Calling it a close question, Blackmun said that by putting the two symbols together, with the secular Christmas tree as the focal point of the display because of its size and placement, and by indicating that the display was a salute to liberty (which can include religious liberty), the city had erected a secular display with a secular purpose.

The crèche was another matter. It is clearly a religious symbol, with the Nativity being a crucial part of the Christian message. And, according to Blackmun, the context made it clear that the county was endorsing that message. Unlike the Nativity scene in *Lynch*, which was surrounded by secular symbols, this Nativity scene was displayed all by itself in the most prominent and beautiful part of the County Courthouse. It was not surrounded by symbols of any other holiday, religious or not, or by secular symbols of Christmas. The angel's banner declared a clearly Christian message, and the poinsettias—which the County argued were a secular symbol—framed and highlighted the crèche rather than distracting from it.

The city won and the county lost. The menorah could stay where it was, surrounded by the Christmas tree and the city sign, but the crèche in the County Courthouse had to be removed.

McCreary County v. ACLU (2005)[5]
In 1999, two Kentucky counties posted large, gold-framed copies of the Ten Commandments in their courthouses. The copies contained part of the King James Version of the Commandments (all ten commandments but omitting the Biblical commentary) and cited Exodus as their source. In McCreary County, the county legislature ordered the Ten Commandments placed in a high traffic area of the courthouse. In Pulaski County, officials hung them in a ceremony that included several references to God.

The ACLU sued to have the displays removed, and the counties responded by adopting resolutions to display a more extensive exhibit. This exhibit surrounded the Ten Commandments with eight other documents, all with religious overtones. They were the national motto, "In God We Trust"; a quote from President Lincoln declaring that "the Bible is the best gift God has ever given to man"; the passage from the Declaration of Independence stating that all men "are endowed, by their Creator, with certain unalienable rights"; the Mayflower Compact; the preamble to Kentucky's constitution; two proclamations that 1983 was the Year of the Bible; and one presidential proclamation designating a National Day of Prayer. The Ten Commandments document was still the largest in the exhibit.

The resolutions for this more extensive display said that the Ten Commandments were "the precedent legal code upon which the civil and criminal codes of ... Kentucky are founded." The resolutions also contained several statements that appeared to endorse religion, including a notation that the Kentucky House of Representatives had adjourned in 1993 "in remembrance and honor of Jesus Christ, the Prince of Ethics'" and a declaration that the founding fathers had an "explicit understanding of the duty of elected officials to publicly acknowledge God as the source of America's strength and direction."

After the District Court told the counties they could not display the second exhibit, they hired new lawyers and changed it one more time. The third exhibit expanded the Exodus quote to include the commentary and replaced some of the surrounding documents. As revised, the exhibit contained copies of the Magna Carta, the Mayflower Compact, the Declaration of Independence, the Bill of Rights, the preamble to the Kentucky constitution, the national motto, the lyrics to "The Star Spangled Banner," and a picture of Lady Justice. The county legislatures did not adopt new resolutions and did not repeal or amend the resolutions authorizing the second display.

Officials for the counties justified the third display by stating that it was intended to educate the counties' citizens by showing them that the Ten Commandments were part of the foundation of the American system of law and government. The District Court found, however, that the history of the two exhibits showed the counties' real purpose was religious rather than secular, and it enjoined the use of the third exhibit. The Sixth Circuit affirmed the injunction.

The Supreme Court agreed with the District Court's analysis. Five justices found that the primary purpose of the third display, as with the first two, was to send a religious message. So it violated the Establishment Clause and could not remain on public property.

The Court usually accepts the government's stated secular purpose unless it is blatantly false. The five justices who joined the Court's decision were not willing to ignore the displays' recent history. In addition, the expansion of the Exodus text and the selection of documents in the third display—which included the Magna Carta and the national anthem but omitted the U.S. Constitution and the Fourteenth Amendment—indicated that the display was not designed to show the foundations of the American legal and political systems.

Van Orden v. Perry (2005)[6]

The Ten Commandments monument that Van Orden walked by on his way to the law library was just one of seventeen monuments and twenty-one historical markers located on the grounds surrounding the Texas State Capitol. It stood in the same place for forty years, having been commissioned and donated by the Fraternal Order of Eagles in 1961.

Although the 40-year-old record was sparse, the District Court concluded that Texas accepted and displayed the monument to recognize and commend the Eagles for their efforts to reduce juvenile delinquency, which it found to be a valid secular purpose. The District Court also found that one passive religious monument among many monuments would not lead a reasonable observer to conclude that Texas was endorsing religion. Therefore, he denied Van Orden's petition to have the monument removed. The Fifth Circuit and the Supreme Court accepted the District Court's findings and affirmed the denial.

Five justices voted to affirm the lower courts' findings that the monument did not violate the Establishment Clause, but only four could agree on the reason. Chief Justice Rehnquist, announcing the opinion of the Court and writing on behalf of himself and Justices Scalia, Kennedy, and Thomas, looked at the monument's nature with a deferential eye to America's religious heritage. As he put it:

> Our institutions presuppose a Supreme Being, yet these institutions must not press religious observances upon their citizens. One face looks to the past in acknowledgment of our Nation's heritage, while the other looks to the present in demanding a separation between church and state. Reconciling these two faces requires that we neither abdicate our responsibility to maintain a division between church and state nor evince a hostility to religion by disabling the government from in some ways recognizing our religious heritage: . . .[7]

So was Chief Justice Rehnquist telling the lower courts that they must consider the country's religious background when deciding Establishment Clause cases? No. He may have been giving them permission to do so, but with nine justices voting, what four of them say is not precedent. It takes a majority to bind the lower courts.

Justice Breyer was the fifth vote. What he said is not precedent, either. But his concurring opinion does provide insight into the thoughts of the justices who carry the deciding votes in Establishment Clause cases.

Breyer pointed out that the Court has not been able to fashion a test that works in every Establishment Clause case. Although the Court has announced some basic principles, how those principles apply may depend on the specific facts in the case. According to Breyer, that requires the justices to exercise legal judgment, especially in borderline cases. He went on to say, however, that the legal judgment he was talking about is not a personal judgment but "must reflect and remain faithful to the underlying purposes of the Clauses." He then said: "While the Court's prior tests provide useful guideposts ... no exact formula can dictate a resolution to such fact-intensive cases." Breyer concluded that the monument's setting, the intent of the donors (a private civic organization that sought to highlight the Ten Commandments' role in shaping morality), and the fact that the monument had generated little opposition in forty years all pointed to its constitutionality.

So Van Orden still walks by the Ten Commandments monument on his way to the law library.

The public display cases show that Breyer's analysis is correct. These cases all depended on their facts. Where a religious message predominated and appeared to be endorsed by government, the Supreme Court found that the display violated the Establishment Clause. Where the religious message was one of many equally prominent secular ones, it did not.

Employment and Tax Cases

The Ten Commandments monument offended Van Orden, but it did not take any money out of his pocket or affect his livelihood. Unlike the public display cases, the employment and tax cases have financial consequences for individuals and private entities.

Walz v. Tax Commission of New York City (1970)[8]

Should taxpaying property owners be required to indirectly subsidize churches? Frederick Walz did not think so. He filed a lawsuit challenging the property tax exemption for churches, alleging that the exemption violated the religion clauses of the First Amendment by forcing taxpayers to indirectly contribute to those churches.

In the 1970 decision, the Supreme Court noted that it has struggled through the years to find a neutral course between the Establishment Clause and the Free Exercise Clause, "both of which are cast in absolute terms, and either of which, if expanded to a logical extreme, would tend to clash with the other."[9] The Court went on to say:

> [W]e will not tolerate either governmentally established religion or governmental interference with religion. Short of those expressly proscribed governmental acts there is room for play in the joints productive of a benevolent neutrality which will permit religious exercise to exist without sponsorship and without interference.[10]

The tax exemption for churches was part of a broader tax exemption that also covered hospitals, libraries, professional organizations, and other nonprofit groups. The Court held that, in these circumstances, the exemption did not violate the Establishment Clause. Therefore, churches continued to be exempt from property taxes.[11]

Estate of Thornton v. Caldor (1985)[12]
Should employers be required to accommodate employees' religious practices even when those practices have a direct (and negative) effect on the employer? Connecticut apparently thought so.

Donald Thornton managed the clothing department in one of Caldor, Inc.'s stores. He started working there when the store was closed on Sundays to comply with Connecticut law. When Connecticut changed the law two years later, Caldor opened the store on Sundays and required its managers to work every third or fourth one. Thornton, who was a Presbyterian, initially complied with Caldor's requirement. Then he discovered that the new law gave employees the right to take their Sabbaths off even if their employers did not want them to. So he told Caldor he would no longer work on Sundays.

Caldor offered to transfer Thornton to a store in Massachusetts that still closed on Sundays or to a lower paying, nonsupervisory position at his current location. Thornton refused, and Caldor demoted him anyway. Thornton then quit and sued Caldor for wrongful discharge. One of Caldor's defenses was that the Sabbath statute violated the Establishment Clause.

The Supreme Court agreed with Caldor. According to the Court, the statute advanced a particular religious practice (Sabbath observance) at the expense of those with different religious practices or with no religion at all. Therefore, it violated the Establishment Clause.

The Connecticut law gave individuals an absolute right not to work on their Sabbath, regardless of their employers' needs. Under the law, if a teacher observed Sabbath on Friday, the school would have to hire someone else to fill in one day a week. If half the employees of a medical clinic observed their Sabbath on the same day, the clinic would either have to close on that day or require the rest of its employees to work then. The statute did not merely require an employer to balance its burden with that of its employee by offering the employee a reasonable accommodation—it required the employer to ignore its own needs entirely.

Would a less onerous statute have survived constitutional scrutiny? It's hard to say. The Court did take time to point out the burdens the statute put on employers, however, so those burdens may have factored into its decision. As it was written, however, the statute was invalid, and employees no longer had an absolute right to take their Sabbaths off.

Corporation of the Presiding Bishop v. Amos (1987)[13]

The Deseret Gymnasium was a nonprofit facility owned and run by two corporations connected with the Mormon Church. By Church policy, all Gymnasium employees were required to qualify for a "temple recommend," which was issued to an individual who attended services regularly, tithed, and behaved consistently with Church doctrine. Frank Mayson failed to qualify after sixteen years as a building engineer at the Gymnasium. Even though he was given a warning and an additional six months, he still failed to qualify, and he was fired.

Mayson sued his employer under a federal statute prohibiting employers from discriminating on the basis of religion. The Corporation of the Presiding Bishop relied on the same statute but used a different section, which stated that the law did not apply to religious entities that hire from within their own religion. Mayson countered that the exemption violates the Establishment Clause when applied to nonreligious jobs.

The Court held that the exemption did not violate the Establishment Clause, even when applied to jobs that are secular in nature. The Court said the exemption alleviated significant government interference with religious organizations' ability to carry out their religious missions, and it held that a government can act to limit the burdens its laws would otherwise place on the exercise of religion. According to the Court, "[a] law is not unconstitutional simply because it allows churches to advance religion, which is their very purpose."

So Mayson lost his job, and religious entities do not have to hire individuals who do not practice the same religion.

Texas Monthly v. Bullock (1989) [14]
Between 1984 and 1987, Texas charged sales tax on magazine subscriptions running a year or longer. It exempted magazines published or distributed by a "religious faith" that were devoted to the faith's teachings.

Texas Monthly published a general interest magazine that did not qualify for the exemption. It paid its 1985 sales taxes under protest and then sued to recover them. It claimed that the sales tax exemption violated the Establishment Clause by discriminating in favor of religious publishers.

The Supreme Court reviewed several previous Establishment Clause cases, including *Walz*, that had upheld laws providing benefits to religious groups. The Court noted, however, that the benefits in these cases flowed to a large number of nonreligious groups as well as to religious groups. The Texas tax exemption, on the other hand, benefited only religious groups. Therefore, the Court held, it violated the Establishment Clause.

Since Texas could not limit the tax exemption to religious groups, Texas Monthly got its sales taxes back. [15]

At first glance, these cases appear to be inconsistent. A property tax exemption for churches was constitutional, while a sales tax exemption for religious publications was not. A provision exempting religious organizations from statutory prohibitions on employment discrimination based on religion was constitutional, but a law requiring employers to give all employees their Sabbath off was not.

At second glance, however, they are not so different. *Walz*, *Corporation of the Presiding Bishop*, and *Texas Monthly* all involved exemptions from obligations that were imposed by the government—taxes in *Waltz* and *Texas Monthly* and no discrimination in *Corporation of the Presiding Bishop*. Without the original laws, no one would have been required to pay taxes and all private entities would have been free to discriminate based on religion. So the exemptions were designed to put the people who received them back in the same place they would have been without the law.

The property tax exemption in *Walz* was available to a broad range of organizations with a common characteristic (i.e., nonprofit status), while the *Texas Monthly* exemption singled out religious publications. The religion-based exemption in *Corporation of the Presiding Bishop* went to the heart of the religious organization's purpose, while the religion-based benefit conferred in *Texas Monthly* did not. And *Estate of Thornton* did not involve an exemption at all but dealt with an attempt to impose a new, religion-based obligation on private employers.

Taken together, these cases show that it is easier to survive an Establishment Clause attack if the challenged provision is an exemption rather than an obligation and if it applies to a broader class than just religion. But, as in *Corporation of the Presiding Bishop*, even laws that benefit religion alone will be upheld against an Establishment Clause challenge if there is a compelling reason for the distinction.

Potpourri

Other significant Establishment Clause cases do not fit neatly into a particular category. But they do provide insight into the Supreme Court's reasoning when interpreting the Establishment Clause and applying it to particular facts.

McGowan v. Maryland (1961)[16]

That day in 1958 started like any other Sunday in Anne Arundel County, Maryland. The seven department store employees were just doing their jobs and selling merchandise to customers: One sold a three-ring loose-leaf binder, one sold a can of floor wax, one sold a stapler, one sold a toy submarine, and the others sold items that were equally harmless. Unfortunately for them, they sold those items to policemen on a mission. The policemen were not looking for criminals selling drugs or guns or other contraband. They were looking for ordinary store clerks selling everyday items in violation of Maryland's Sunday closing law.

Maryland, Pennsylvania, Massachusetts, and several other New England states had laws, commonly known as "blue laws," that prohibited most businesses from being open on Sunday. These laws were originally adopted in colonial times, when they were clearly designed to compel church attendance and to keep the Christian Sabbath holy. Over the years, however, the Sunday closing laws became riddled with exceptions. In Maryland, for example, stores could sell tobacco, candy, and souvenirs but not office supplies or toys. The law prohibited some recreational businesses, such as opera houses and bowling alleys, from operating on Sundays, but it allowed local exceptions. In Anne Arundel County, dancing saloons could stay open on Sundays and people could play slot machines, pinball machines, and bingo.

The Supreme Court found that the religious purposes of the Sunday Closing Laws had been replaced with recreational ones: to give employees time for recreation and to ensure that families had one day a week they could spend together. Simply requiring employers to give each employee one day off a week would have satisfied the first recreational purpose but not the second since family members might not have the same day off. Chief Justice Warren, speaking for the majority, summed it up this way:

The present purpose and effect of [the Sunday Closing Laws] is to provide a uniform day of rest for all citizens; the fact that this day is Sunday, a day of particular significance for the dominant Christian sects, does not bar the State from achieving its secular goals. To say that the States cannot prescribe Sunday as a day of rest for these purposes solely because centuries ago such laws had their genesis in religion would give a constitutional interpretation of hostility to the public welfare rather than one of mere separation of church and State.[17]

The Supreme Court held that the Sunday closing laws did not violate the Establishment Clause since they no longer had a religious purpose. As a result, the department store employees could not sell office supplies and toys on Sundays, and their convictions stood.

The holding in these cases was not new. In *Hennington v. Georgia* (1896), which affirmed Hennington's conviction for running a freight train through Georgia on Sunday, the Court said:

That which is properly made a civil duty by statute is none the less so because it is also a real or supposed religious obligation … . Doubtless it is a religious duty to pay debts, but no one supposes that this is any obstacle to its being exacted as a civil duty. With few exceptions, the same may be said of the whole catalogue of duties specified in the Ten Commandments. Those of them which are purely and exclusively religious in their nature cannot be made civil duties, but all the rest may be … . There is a wide difference between keeping a day holy as a religious observance, and merely forbearing to labor on that day in one's ordinary vocation or business pursuit.[18]

Torcaso v. Watkins (1961)[19]
Roy Torcaso wanted to be a notary public in Maryland, and he met all the qualifications. Except one. Torcaso refused to say he believed in God.

The Maryland Constitution prohibited the use of any religious test "other than a declaration of belief in the existence of

God" to qualify for an official position in the state. When Torcaso refused to declare his belief in God, state officials refused to let him be a notary public. But Torcaso claimed that the declaration violated the religion clauses of the First Amendment.

The Supreme Court agreed with Torcaso. Although the Court did not specifically mention the Establishment Clause, it held that a government cannot constitutionally force anyone to profess a belief or disbelief in any religion or impose requirements that "aid all religions as against non-believers" or "aid those religions based on a belief in the existence of God as against those religions founded on different beliefs."[20] This is clearly an Establishment Clause result.

Since the oath requirement was unconstitutional, Torcaso could be a notary public without claiming to believe in God.

Larson v. Valente (1982)[21]

Minnesota's Charitable Solicitations Act required charities to register with the Minnesota Department of Commerce and file annual financial reports containing detailed information. All religious organizations were exempt until 1978. Then Minnesota amended the Act to exempt only those religious organizations that received more than half of their contributions from their own members.

The Unification Church did not qualify. It received more than 50 percent of its contributions from going door-to-door and soliciting funds in public places. After the law was amended, the Department of Commerce notified the Unification Church that it must register and file financial reports. Several members then sued.

Justice Brennan, writing for the Supreme Court majority, stated that: "The clearest command of the Establishment Clause is that one religious denomination cannot be officially preferred over another."[22] The Court found that the 50 percent rule violated the Establishment Clause by discriminating among religions and denominations. Therefore, the Unification Church was free to solicit without registering or filing financial statements.

Larkin v. Grendel's Den (1982)[23]

Grendel's Den applied for a liquor license for a restaurant in Cambridge, Massachusetts, but it had a problem. A state law gave churches, schools, hospitals, and similar institutions the right to veto any liquor license application filed by an establishment located within 500 feet. Grendel's Den was located right behind Holy Cross Church, which objected to the license. After exhausting its administrative remedies, Grendel's Den sued and asked the court to order the Cambridge License Commission to give it a liquor license.

The Supreme Court recognized that the state had a valid secular purpose in protecting spiritual, cultural, and educational institutions from the noise and public disturbances that alcohol can cause. The Court did not take issue with the state's ends, just with its means. Chief Justice Burger stated in his opinion for the Court that the Massachusetts law "substitutes the unilateral and absolute power of a church for the reasoned decision-making of a public legislative body acting on evidence and guided by standards, on issues with significant economic and political implications."[24] Because Massachusetts had delegated its discretionary powers to religious organizations, the statute violated the Establishment Clause.

Could Massachusetts have adopted a zoning law that simply banned all liquor sales within 500 feet of a church? Maybe. Or a zoning board could have held public hearings and considered the church's views—along with Grendel's Den's views and the views of other neighbors—when reaching its decision. But the government could not hand its zoning decisions over to a church. So Grendel's Den got its liquor license and became a popular hangout on Harvard Square.

In this potpourri of Establishment Clause cases, the Supreme Court ruled that government may not discriminate in favor of religion (*Larkin*), may not discriminate against those with no religion (*Torcaso*), and may not discriminate between religions

(*Larson*). The Court also held that the mere fact that a law is consistent with a particular religious practice does not mean it violates the Establishment Clause (*McGowan*).

The Establishment Clause as a Defense

Governments often use the Establishment Clause as an excuse for discriminating against religious groups. This defense is seldom successful, even when the government acts on a good faith belief that the Establishment Clause requires the discrimination. This is especially true where the discrimination clashes with the free exercise and free speech rights discussed in later chapters.[25]

So what do the cases described in this chapter and Chapter 6 say about the Establishment Clause? First, the purpose test is a significant factor in the Court's decisions. If the purpose of the law is to endorse a particular religion or religion in general; to oppose a particular religion or religion in general; or to discriminate in favor of, against, or among religions, it violates the Establishment Clause. If the government claims a valid secular purpose, however, the Court usually accepts the government's claim unless it defies logic.

Second, the Establishment Clause allows aid to religious institutions for secular purposes where the aid is also available to nonreligious institutions on a reasonably similar basis. If public school children receive the use of free textbooks for secular academic subjects, parochial school children can too. If hospitals and libraries receive tax exemptions for property used for nonprofit purposes, churches can too.

... the mere fact that a law is consistent with a particular religion's beliefs or practices does not make it unconstitutional.

Third, the mere fact that a law is consistent with a particular religion's beliefs or practices does not make it unconstitutional. Sunday closing laws are just as valid as Tuesday closing laws as long as they have a current secular purpose unrelated to religion.

Finally, the Supreme Court has recognized a no-man's-land between the Establishment Clause and the Free Exercise Clause. The Establishment Clause does not prevent governments from taking steps to ease the burdens the state itself has imposed, nor is it an excuse for denying religious rights guaranteed by the Free Exercise Clause. Those rights are the subject of the next chapter.

Question 1: Was the Supreme Court correct when it concluded that the Sunday closing laws no longer serve a primarily religious purpose? What facts support your conclusion?

Question 2: Review the second hypothetical case in Chapter 1 (A Town with Heart). Based on the public display cases in this chapter, would the Court allow Heart to put a statue of Mother Theresa in the town square? Why or why not?

CHAPTER EIGHT
WHEN INTERESTS COLLIDE

William Gobitis was so incorrigible that he was expelled from school when he was ten. What was his crime? Bringing a gun to school? Threatening a teacher? Bullying his classmates? No. William's crime was much worse. He stood in respectful silence while the rest of the school saluted the flag and recited the Pledge of Allegiance.

In 1935, the flag salute was a purely patriotic exercise without any religious overtones. Even the words "under God" would not be added to the Pledge for almost twenty years. But William was a Jehovah's Witness, and he believed that saluting anything other than God violated the second commandment.[1]

When William refused to salute the flag, he had no idea that he was about to receive a real-life civics lesson on the Free Exercise Clause of the First Amendment. That clause says "Congress shall make no law ... prohibiting the free exercise [of religion]."

oth the Establishment Clause and the Free Exercise Clause place restraints on government action, but they each have a different focus. In general, the Establishment Clause governs what must be prohibited while the Free Exercise Clause governs what must be allowed. Government cannot pass laws prohibiting the free exercise of religion. But what does that mean? Is the right to free exercise absolute? Must Congress and the states allow human sacrifice? Can they require everyone to salute the flag or obtain and use a Social Security number? This chapter will show where the U.S. Supreme Court has drawn the line in protecting religiously motivated conduct.

The Jehovah's Witness Cases
William Gobitis's case was one of a string of Jehovah's Witness cases to come before the U.S. Supreme Court in the World War II years. Many Americans despised the Jehovah's Witnesses

because they were vocal critics of organized religion—particularly the Roman Catholic Church, which they called an instrument of Satan.[2]

In an era of intense patriotism, the Witnesses' refusal to salute the flag heightened the prejudice against them. The flag salute controversy resulted in school expulsions and lawsuits all over the country. Two of those cases made it all the way to the Supreme Court.

Minersville School District v. Gobitis (1940)[3]
The Minersville School District expelled William and his older sister Lillian for refusing to salute the flag. Since Pennsylvania made school attendance compulsory and the public schools had banned them, they were forced to attend a private school. But private schools cost money, so William and Lillian's father sued, asking the courts to order the school district to reimburse him and to accept his children back in the public schools without requiring them to salute the flag.

The Court weighed the children's free exercise rights against national unity, and national unity won. After extolling the importance of the Free Exercise Clause and stating that "every possible leeway should be given to claims of religious faith," the Court said that national unity was "an interest inferior to none in the hierarchy of legal values."[4]

The Court concluded that it would not substitute its judgment for the school board's judgment on how to instill that unity in school children. Then it upheld William's and Lillian's expulsions.

Justice Stone was the lone dissent. He agreed that government has the right to adopt general laws not aimed at religion or any particular religious group, to require individuals without conscientious objections to comply with those laws, and even to enforce certain laws against individuals with religious scruples where doing so is necessary for public safety, health, or good order. Justice Stone disagreed, however, on where government can draw the line to sanction religiously motivated disobedience:

> [W]hile such expressions of loyalty, when voluntarily given, may promote national unity, it is quite another matter to say that their compulsory expression by children in violation of their own and their parents' religious convictions can be regarded as playing so important a part in our national unity as to leave school boards free to exact it despite the constitutional guarantee of freedom of religion. The very terms of the Bill of Rights preclude, it seems to me, any reconciliation of such compulsions with the constitutional guaranties by a legislative declaration that they are more important to the public welfare than the Bill of Rights.[5]

West Virginia State Board of Education v. Barnette (1943)[6]

Three years after *Gobitis* was decided, Justice Stone—who was now Chief Justice Stone—voted with the majority in another case where a school expelled Jehovah's Witness students for refusing to salute the flag. Chief Justice Stone was not the one who changed his mind, however.

This time the Court decided that the Free Exercise Clause trumped national unity, and it overruled the *Gobitis* decision by a 6–3 vote. Hugo Black, William O. Douglas, and Frank Murphy changed their votes and joined Chief Justice Stone, and two new justices voted with them.[7]

Events happening outside of the Court may have played a role in its change of direction. Within days after *Gobitis* was decided, the country erupted in a series of violent, and well publicized, attacks on Jehovah's Witnesses.[8] Did Justices Black, Douglas, and Murphy wonder if their decision had sparked national division rather than national unity? Whatever the cause, their second thoughts swung the case in the Witnesses' favor.

By 1943, the justices had concluded that allowing school children to stand quietly during the flag salute did not create the kind of danger to society that would justify their expulsion. Justice Jackson, who wrote the Court's opinion, saw the issue as freedom of speech more than freedom of religion. According to Justice Jackson:

> [H]ere the power of compulsion is invoked without any allegation that remaining passive during a flag salute ritual creates a clear

> and present danger that would justify an effort even to muffle
> expression. To sustain the compulsory flag salute we are required
> to say that a Bill of Rights which guards the individual's right to
> speak his own mind, left it open to public authorities to compel
> him to utter what is not in his mind.[9]

Justices Black, Douglas, and Murphy, while agreeing with
the Court's opinion, put more emphasis on the freedom of
religion aspects of the case. In a concurring opinion, Justice
Murphy put it this way:

> [T]here is before us the right of freedom to believe, freedom to
> worship one's Maker according to the dictates of one's conscience,
> a right which the Constitution specifically shelters. Reflection has
> convinced me that as a judge I have no loftier duty or responsibility
> than to uphold that spiritual freedom to its farthest reaches.[10]

The flag salute cases were a small part of the Jehovah's Witness
cases that made it to the Supreme Court around the time of
World War II. One group of Jehovah's Witness cases arose from
local restrictions on selling or distributing religious literature
and soliciting contributions, which they claimed their religion
required.[11] Most of these cases are primarily freedom of speech
cases and are discussed in a later chapter, but two are worth
mentioning here.

Cantwell v. Connecticut (1940) is a typical case.[12] Newton
Cantwell and his two sons, Jesse and Russell, were arrested in
New Haven, Connecticut, and found guilty of violating a city ordinance requiring them to get a license before soliciting funds.
New Haven's licensing ordinance gave a city official authority
to determine which groups were bona fide charitable or religious organizations and to deny licenses to the rest. Since the
Cantwells' religion required that they witness and solicit funds,
they argued that the license requirements, and their convictions, violated the Free Exercise Clause.

Justice Roberts' decision for the Court contains a statement quoted in almost every subsequent Free Exercise case:

> Thus the Amendment embraces two concepts—freedom to believe and freedom to act. The first is absolute but, in the nature of things, the second cannot be. Conduct remains subject to regulation for the protection of society.[13]

Nonetheless, the Court vacated the convictions because the ordinance allowed a city official to determine whether a particular religion is "bona fide."

In *Prince v. Massachusetts* (1944), Sarah Prince took her niece with her to sell religious magazines on the street.[14] Nine-year-old Betty was a willing seller who believed that God had commanded her to distribute the literature and who called it her way of worshiping God. But Massachusetts did not care what either Betty or her aunt believed. In its eyes, Betty was just a child, and her aunt was violating the child labor laws.

Although the Supreme Court had agreed with the Jehovah's Witnesses in other cases involving the sale of religious literature, it agreed with the state on this one. The difference was in the interest that government sought to protect. In the cases the Witnesses won, the government sought to protect other citizens from being bothered by unwanted solicitations or from walking on streets littered with discarded handbills. In this case, the government sought to protect a child's welfare. The Court found that a state could limit parental freedom and authority when a child's welfare was at stake, and it affirmed Sarah Prince's conviction for violating the child labor laws.

The Court did, however, limit its ruling to the facts of the case. According to Justice Rutledge:

> We neither lay the foundation "for any [that is, every] state intervention in the indoctrination and participation of children in religion" which may be done "in the name of their health and welfare" nor give warrant for "every limitation on their religious training and activities." The religious training and indoctrination

of children may be accomplished in many ways, some of which, as we have noted, have received constitutional protection through decisions of this Court. These ... remain unaffected by the decision.[15]

The other group of cases arose from the Jehovah's Witnesses' attempts to meet in public places.[16] The 1951 case of *Niemotko v. Maryland* is a typical example.[17] The city of Harve de Grace denied the Witnesses' request for a permit to hold a meeting in the park even though it had allowed other religious groups to meet there. The Supreme Court concluded that the city council violated the Witnesses' First Amendment rights by intentionally discriminating against them because of their religious beliefs. The opinion noted that the questions asked by city council members at the permit hearing had nothing to do with the peaceful use of the park but keyed in on other issues, including the Witnesses' refusal to salute the flag. So that issue was still haunting them almost a decade after the Court reversed *Gobitis*.

The Mormon Polygamy Cases

The Jehovah's Witnesses were not the first to challenge government action under the Free Exercise Clause. The Mormons were. The Supreme Court confronted the clause head-on for the first time in the 1878 case of *Reynolds v. U.S.*[18]

The Territory of Utah convicted George Reynolds of bigamy. He argued that it was his religious duty as a Mormon to practice polygamy and that the territorial government could not convict him for fulfilling his religious duty.

Although the justices recognized that the Free Exercise Clause applied within the territories as well as within the states, they unanimously held that it did not protect the Mormon practice. Writing for the Court, Chief Justice Waite stated:

Laws are made for the government of actions, and while they cannot interfere with mere religious belief and opinions, they may with practices. Suppose one believed that human sacrifices were a necessary part of religious worship, would it be seriously contented that the civil government under which he lived could not interfere to prevent a sacrifice? Or if a wife religiously believed it was her duty to burn herself upon the funeral pile of her dead husband, would it be beyond the power of the civil government to prevent her carrying her belief into practice?

So here, as a law of the organization of society under the exclusive dominion of the United States, it is provided that plural marriages shall not be allowed. Can a man excuse his practices to the contrary because of his religious belief? To permit this would be to make the professed doctrines of religious belief superior to the law of the land, and in effect to permit every citizen to become a law unto himself. Government could exist only in name under such circumstances.[19]

Twelve years after it upheld Reynolds' conviction for bigamy, the Supreme Court decided *Davis v. Beason* (1890) and upheld the conviction of another Mormon, this time for perjury.[20] Utah law said that no one could vote in territorial elections unless he took an oath that he did not belong to any group that taught or practiced polygamy. This created a dilemma for Davis. He had three choices: relinquish the right to vote, change his religion, or lie. Davis chose to lie.

The Court had no sympathy for Davis's dilemma. In its collective mind, approval of polygamy was as infamous as the actual practice. Therefore, Davis's conviction stood and Mormons were deprived of the right to vote.[21]

Later that same year, the Supreme Court decided *Late Corporation of the Church of Jesus Christ of Latter-Day Saints v. U.S.*[22] In the 1850s the Mormon Church established a corporation to own property. In 1887, the United States dissolved the corporation and seized all of its property, except its worship facilities, because the Mormons had defied the laws prohibiting polygamy.

The Supreme Court agreed with the government. The strong language in Justice Bradley's majority opinion reflects a deep-seated distrust of the Mormon Church and its motives:

> One pretense for this obstinate course is, that their belief in the practice of polygamy, or in the right to indulge in it, is a religious belief, and, therefore, under the protection of the constitutional guaranty of religious freedom. This is altogether a sophistical plea. No doubt the Thugs of India imagined that their belief in the right of assassination was a religious belief; but their thinking so did not make it so .... The offering of human sacrifices by our own ancestors in Britain was no doubt sanctioned by an equally conscientious impulse. But no one, on that account, would hesitate to brand these practices, now, as crimes against society, and obnoxious to condemnation and punishment by the civil authority.
>
> The state has a perfect right to prohibit polygamy, and all other open offenses against the enlightened sentiment of mankind, notwithstanding the pretense of religious conviction by which they may be advocated and practiced.[23]

By 1946, mainstream Mormons had become monogamous. But one group continued to practice polygamy, and federal prosecutors convicted several of its members of transporting women across state lines for immoral purposes. The Court upheld those convictions for the same reasons it gave sixty years earlier.[24]

Much of the once widespread prejudice against the Mormons and their religious practices has disappeared, and the Supreme Court has softened its view of the relationship between religion and manmade laws since the late 1800s. But the basic principle behind these cases remains. The Court has never wavered from its conviction that the Free Exercise Clause is absolute when it comes to protecting religious beliefs but not when it comes to protecting religiously motivated conduct.

When There is No Government Actor

In the Jehovah's Witness and Mormon cases, it was clearly the government itself that prohibited the conduct the religious groups wanted to engage in. But what if the government is acting on behalf of someone else? That was the situation in *Reuben Quick Bear v. Leupp* (1908).[25]

The Secretary of the Interior administered the Sioux tribe's treaty trust funds, and he paid some of them to the St. Francis Mission Boarding School on the Rosebud Reservation in South Dakota. Reuben Quick Bear objected, apparently claiming that using the trust—which was funded with public monies—to subsidize a Roman Catholic school violated the spirit of the Constitution.

The Court held that the opposite was true. The money in the trust fund belonged to the Sioux even though the Secretary of the Interior administered it. According to Chief Justice Fuller, depriving the Sioux of the right to use their money to educate their children in the schools of their choice would violate their free exercise rights.

Laws Relating to Religious Practices

So when does the Free Exercise Clause protect religiously motivated conduct? Part of it depends on the purpose of the law. As the following cases show, a law or prohibition targeted at religious (or irreligious) conduct will rarely survive a Free Exercise challenge.

Torcaso v. Watkins (1961)[26]

Torcaso was appointed a notary public in Maryland but could not get the actual commission because he refused to declare that he believed in God. As discussed in a previous chapter, the Supreme Court held that the religious qualification violated the Establishment Clause. But it also held that the religious test invaded Torcaso's freedom of belief and religion as protected by the Free Exercise Clause.

Cruz v. Beto (1972)[27]

Cruz was incarcerated in a Texas prison. He claimed that he was a Buddhist and that prison officials denied him privileges extended to prisoners from other religions. In particular, he alleged that he was not allowed to use the prison chapel, to correspond with his religious advisor, or to share his Buddhist materials with other inmates, while Christians and Jews were allowed to do all of those and were even provided with prison chaplains at government expense.

Since the lower courts dismissed the case without hearing any evidence, the Supreme Court was required to accept the allegations as true for the time being. Looking at those allegations, the Court stated:

> If Cruz was a Buddhist and if he was denied a reasonable opportunity of pursuing his faith comparable to the opportunity afforded fellow prisoners who adhere to conventional religious precepts, then there was palpable discrimination by the State against the Buddhist religion, established 600 B.C., long before the Christian era ... . If the allegations of this complaint are assumed to be true, as they must be on the motion to dismiss, Texas has violated the First and Fourteenth Amendments.[28]

So the case went back to the trial court for a hearing on Cruz's allegations.

McDaniel v. Paty (1978)[29]

McDaniel was a Baptist minister in Tennessee. When Tennessee decided to hold a state constitutional convention, McDaniel wanted to be a delegate. He filed to run in the election, but one of his opponents, Paty, did not want the competition. So Paty sued to strike McDaniel's name from the ballot because state law said that clergy were ineligible. The election took place before the case reached the Supreme Court, and McDaniel beat Paty—and the other candidates—by a wide margin.

The Court agreed with the voters. All eight justices who participated in the case found the Tennessee law unconstitutional. Three justices relied on *Torcaso*, and four said *Torcaso* was irrelevant because it focused on the individual's belief while the Tennessee law focused on the individual's status, acts, and conduct (in becoming a minister). Even so, seven justices found that the law violated the Free Exercise Clause.[30]

Church of Lukumi Babalu Aye, Inc. v. City of Hialeah (1993)[31]

Ernesto Pichardo was a priest for the Church of Lukumi Babalu Aye, which practiced Santeria ("the way of the saints"). Members of the Santeria religion sacrifice animals—chickens, pigeons, doves, ducks, guinea pigs, goats, sheep, and turtles—at important events (e.g., births, marriages, and deaths), to cure the sick, and during an annual celebration. The animals are killed by cutting their neck arteries, and after the sacrifice the congregation cooks and eats them (except after healing and death rituals).

The Santeria religion came to southern Florida from Africa by way of Cuba, where persecution drove it underground. Now Pichardo wanted to give his congregation a place to practice openly. So the church obtained land in the city of Hialeah, Florida, and began the process of obtaining the necessary city permits for its church. Although the city eventually granted the necessary permits, many citizens were openly hostile to the religion. So the city council bowed to political pressure and passed several ordinances that were phrased as general ordinances regarding sanitation issues and cruelty to animals but were carefully crafted to ensure that only the Santeria sacrifices were affected. In particular, the ordinances exempted slaughter for commercial purposes and kosher slaughter, which—like Santeria sacrifice—kills the animals by cutting their carotid arteries.

As in *McDaniel*, the justices were unanimous in declaring the ordinances unconstitutional but were divided in their reasons. Nonetheless, the majority agreed on one principle: "A law that targets religious conduct for distinctive treatment or advances legitimate governmental interests only against conduct with a religious motivation will survive strict scrutiny only in rare cases."[32] The Court not only found that this was not one of those cases, but Justice Kennedy's opinion used strong language to condemn the actions of the Hialeah city officials:

Legislators may not devise mechanisms, overt or disguised, designed to persecute or oppress a religion or its practices.

The Free Exercise Clause commits government itself to religious tolerance, and upon even slight suspicion that proposals for state intervention stem from animosity to religion or distrust of its practices, all officials must pause to remember their own high duty to the Constitution and to the rights it secures. Those in office must be resolute in resisting importunate demands and must ensure that the sole reasons for imposing the burdens of law and regulation are secular. Legislators may not devise mechanisms, overt or disguised, designed to persecute or oppress a religion or its practices. The laws here in question were enacted contrary to these constitutional principles, and they are void.[33]

As the Court recognized in *Church of Lukumi Babalu Aye*, even targeted laws may be valid in rare cases. The polygamy laws in the Utah territory were probably adopted with the Mormons in mind. Still, they prohibited polygamy by everyone; they were not written to catch Mormons and exclude others. The Court also found that the practice created a significant threat to public safety, peace, and order and resulted in significant harm to women—particularly the Mormon wives.

Locke v. Davey (2004) is another case where the Court upheld a targeted law.[34] Joshua Davey graduated from a public high school in the State of Washington. He qualified for a Promise Scholarship: a state scholarship available to qualified students who attended college within the state. But there was a problem. Davey wanted to train for the ministry while receiving the scholarship, and the scholarship was not available to theology students.

The Court held that the Promise Scholarship fit within the "play in the joints" between the Establishment Clause and the Free Exercise Clause. Chief Justice Rehnquist spoke for seven of the justices when he said:

"Far from evincing the hostility toward religion which was manifest in *Lukumi*, we believe that the entirety of the Promise Scholarship Program goes a long way toward including religion in its benefits. The program permits students to attend pervasively religious schools, so long as they are accredited ... . And under the Promise Scholarship Program's current guidelines, students are still eligible to take devotional theology courses ..."

Without a presumption of unconstitutionality, Davey's claim must fail. The State's interest in not funding the pursuit of devotional degrees is substantial and the exclusion of such funding places a relatively minor burden on Promise Scholars. If any room exists between the two Religion Clauses, it must be here.

Davey did not get a Promise Scholarship, and he did not enter the ministry, either. His experience with the court system convinced him that God was calling him to be a lawyer rather than a pastor, and he went on to study at Harvard Law School.[35]

Secular Laws That Apply to Society in General

The standard is lower when a government adopts a neutral law designed to achieve valid secular goals. The stronger the governmental interest, the more likely the law is to survive a First Amendment challenge, especially if the individual's religion does not actually require the prohibited conduct or prohibit the required conduct.

Does the individual's religion require or prohibit the conduct?
There is no free exercise right for conduct that is strictly voluntary. Two of the 1961 Sunday closing law cases involved merchants who were Orthodox Jews.[36] The merchants claimed that they needed to be open one day during the weekend or they would not make enough money to stay in business. Since their religion prohibited them from doing business on Friday evening and Saturday, they were left with Sunday. But the Sunday closing laws took that day away as well.

The Supreme Court found that the Sunday closing laws did not violate the merchants' free exercise rights. It reiterated its finding that the Sunday closing laws, while originally religious in nature, had become secular with time and now had a valid secular purpose (to provide a uniform day of rest that families can spend together). Then it noted that the laws did not re-

quire the merchants to keep their stores open on Saturday—
which would have violated their religious laws—but merely to
keep them closed on Sunday. Although closing their stores on
Sunday created an economic hardship for the merchants, it
did not conflict with their religion because nothing in the Orthodox Jewish faith required them to work on Sundays.

The Court reached a similar result in *Hernandez v. Commis-
sioner of Internal Revenue*.[37] In this case, members of the Church
of Scientology challenged the IRS's decision that their payments to branch churches were not tax-deductible contributions. The tax laws provided that gift contributions to charitable and religious organizations were tax-deductible but that
payments for goods and services were not. The members paid
for services that—according to the tenets of Scientology—were
necessary for spiritual growth. However, the churches had a set
schedule of fees for the services they provided, and they did
not waive or lower those fees for anyone.

After finding that the payments were not contributions within the meaning of the tax laws, the Court went on to address
the members' First Amendment claims. The Court held that
denying the tax deduction did not violate the Free Exercise
Clause because it did not interfere with the members' ability to
practice their religion; it just made it more expensive because
they could not deduct the payments from their taxes.[38]

There is also no free exercise right if the person has a reasonable alternative that violates neither the law nor that person's religious convictions. In *Tony & Susan Alamo Foundation
v. Secretary of Labor* (1985), the Court found that the minimum
wage laws did not burden religious conduct.[39] The foundation
was a nonprofit religious organization that funded its religious
activities from its many commercial enterprises. Those businesses were staffed mostly by "associates"—recovering alcohol-
ics and drug users who had been rehabilitated by the foundation—who received room, board, clothing, and other benefits
but not money. Several associates testified at trial and classified
themselves as volunteers who were working at the foundation
for religious reasons. Because they depended on it to supply

their needs, however, the trial court found that they were employees rather than volunteers.

The foundation and its officers claimed that the minimum wage laws violated the associates' free exercise rights to volunteer their time to serve God. In rejecting this defense, the Supreme Court noted that the law did not prohibit the associates from contributing their wages back to the foundation as long as they did so voluntarily. Since there was an easy way around the associates' religious objection, the foundation had to comply with the minimum wage laws.

Similarly, the Free Exercise Clause does not protect religious conduct if the religious objectors are not required to comply with the law. In *Hamilton v. Regents of the University of California* (1934), students at the University of California objected to the university's mandatory military training course.[40] The students were members of the Methodist Episcopal Church, which believed that war, and even training for war, was immoral. The Court upheld the military training requirement because enrollment at the university was voluntary. The students could avoid the conflict simply by going to another school.

On the other hand, the religious obligation can be implied, strongly encouraged, or even just a sincerely held conviction. While it cannot be purely voluntary, neither does it have to be an absolute requirement or prohibition.

In *Thomas v. Review Board* (1981), a Jehovah's Witness was hired to work in an Indiana roll foundry that made steel for industrial uses.[41] The roll foundry closed down about a year later, and Thomas's employer transferred him to another facility that produced turrets for military tanks. He had religious scruples about producing military weapons, but those were the only positions available. So Thomas quit and applied for unemployment benefits, which Indiana denied.

Other Jehovah's Witnesses produced military weapons, and it was not clear whether Thomas's religion actually prohibited him from doing so. But the Court refused to decide that question. As Chief Justice Burger stated for the Court:

> The determination of what is a "religious" belief or practice is more often than not a difficult and delicate task … . However, the resolution of that question is not to turn upon a judicial perception of the particular belief or practice in question; religious beliefs need not be acceptable, logical, consistent, or comprehensible to others in order to merit First Amendment protection.[42]

Since Thomas's belief was sincere, he was entitled to unemployment benefits.

In *Frazee v. Illinois Employment Security Dept.* (1989), Illinois denied unemployment compensation to an individual who refused to work on Sundays, which he characterized as "the Lord's Day."[43] Although Frazee said he was a Christian, he did not claim to be a member of a denomination that prohibited its members from working on Sunday. In fact, he didn't claim to belong to any denomination. The state denied benefits because it felt that a belief qualified as "religious" only if the individual's denomination or sect dictated it. But the Supreme Court viewed it differently. As in *Thomas*, the Court was not willing to substitute its own judgment for Frazee's judgment, nor would it let Illinois do so. Frazee believed he could not work on Sundays for religious reasons, and that was enough.

The Court has also held in a different context that it is the sincerity of the beliefs rather than their truth that controls the outcome of litigation. In *United States v. Ballard* (1944), the founders of the "I Am" movement were convicted of fraud in soliciting members and donations.[44] Fraud requires bad faith, so the judge told the jury that it must decide whether the founders believed their religious claims. He also told the jury that they could not look at whether the religious claims were actually true.

The Court agreed with the judge's instruction to the jury. According to Justice Douglas, writing for the Court:

> Men may believe what they cannot prove … . The miracles of the
> New Testament, the Divinity of Christ, life after death, the power of
> prayer are deep in the religious convictions of many. If one could
> be sent to jail because a jury in a hostile environment found those
> teachings false, little indeed would be left of religious freedom.[45]

Because the jury had considered only the defendants' good
faith, and not the truth or falsity of their religious claims, the
convictions stood.

Does the law serve a compelling governmental purpose?
Another factor the Court has looked at is whether the law
serves a compelling governmental purpose. In *Frazee,* Indiana
claimed that allowing people to leave their jobs for "personal
reasons" would create widespread unemployment and put an
economic burden on the fund. *Frazee* was just one in a string
of unemployment compensation cases claiming that denying
benefits served an important government purpose.[46] *Sherbert v.
Verner* (1963) was the first of these cases.[47]

Adell Sherbert was a Seventh-Day Adventist. She worked in a
textile mill until it changed from a 5-day work week to a 6-day
work week. When she refused to work on Saturdays, the mill
fired her. Sherbert attempted to find a job at the other textile
mills in the area but ran into the same problem with Saturday work. She then filed for unemployment benefits. Although
Sherbert was willing to accept any job that did not require her
to work on Saturdays, that was not good enough for the South
Carolina Employment Security Commission. It found that she
had failed to accept suitable employment without good cause
and denied the benefits.

South Carolina claimed that paying benefits might encourage people to file fraudulent claims based on phony religious
objections to Saturday work. These fraudulent claims could
dilute the unemployment compensation fund and could also
make it harder for employers to schedule employees to work
on Saturdays.

The U.S. Supreme Court noted that there was no evidence
in the record to show that South Carolina's fear was justified.

It then found that the denial violated the First Amendment. As Justice Brennan stated in his opinion for the Court, "to condition the availability of benefits upon [Sherbert's] willingness to violate a cardinal principle of her religious faith effectively penalizes the free exercise of her constitutional liberties."[48] The state's justification for its action was insufficient to override Sherbert's First Amendment rights.

Hobbie v. Unemployment Appeals Commission of Florida (1987) also involved a Seventh-Day Adventist who was denied unemployment compensation because she would not work on Saturdays.[49] Hobbie's job as assistant manager of a jewelry store included Saturday hours, and she worked them without objection. Then she became a Seventh-Day Adventist, refused to work on Saturdays, and was fired. Whereas Sherbert's employer changed Sherbert's working conditions to conflict with her religion, Hobbie changed her religion to conflict with her working conditions. In denying Hobbie unemployment compensation, Florida said this difference was important. The Supreme Court disagreed and required Florida to pay the benefits.

The Court also found the state's interest insufficient in *Wisconsin v. Yoder* (1972).[50] Wisconsin law required parents to send their children to school until they turned sixteen. The Amish believed that sending teenagers to high school would endanger their salvation by taking them out of their supportive community during their formative teenage years and exposing them to pressure to conform to worldly ways. Frieda Yoder, Barbara Miller, and Vernon Yutzy stopped attending school after eighth grade even though they were still under sixteen. So Wisconsin arrested their fathers and convicted them of violating the compulsory attendance laws.

The fathers claimed Wisconsin's actions violated their rights under the Free Exercise Clause. Wisconsin, on the other hand, claimed that it had an overriding interest in preparing children to be productive members of society. Chief Justice Burger, writing for the Court, acknowledged the state's interest but found that the informal vocational training provided by the Amish achieved the same goal. The Court also reiterated its finding from earlier cases that parents have a right to guide the religious education of their children, and something more than a reasonable state interest is required before a state can interfere with a parent's decision. Therefore, the fathers' convictions were overturned, and Frieda, Barbara, and Vernon were excused from attending high school.

On the other hand, the Supreme Court has upheld general laws in a number of cases. In *United States v. Lee* (1982), Edwin Lee hired several of his Amish brethren to work on his farm and in his carpentry shop.[51] The Old Order Amish believed that they should take care of their own, so they opposed Social Security. Lee did not file quarterly Social Security tax returns, did not withhold Social Security taxes, and did not pay the employer's share of those taxes. When the Internal Revenue Service tried to collect them, Lee took the case to court, claiming that the Social Security taxes violated his rights under the Free Exercise Clause.

According to the Supreme Court, the United States had an overriding interest in ensuring the Social Security system was financially sound. Allowing people to opt out on behalf of their employees would put the entire system at risk. So even though paying Social Security taxes was against Lee's religious beliefs, the justices unanimously found that the government could collect those taxes without violating the First Amendment.

The Court also found a compelling interest in *Bob Jones University v. United States* (1983).[52] Bob Jones University believed the Bible prohibited interracial dating and marriage, so it denied admission to anyone who was part of an interracial couple or who advocated the practice. The IRS did not care why the university engaged in racially discriminatory conduct, however; it revoked the university's tax-exempt status and announced that contributions were no longer deductible.

The Supreme Court found that the government's interest justified its actions. As Chief Justice Burger stated in the opinion of the Court:

> [T]he Government has a fundamental, overriding interest in eradicating racial discrimination in education ... . That governmental interest substantially outweighs whatever burden denial of tax benefits places on petitioners' exercise of their religious beliefs. The interests asserted by petitioners cannot be accommodated with that compelling governmental interest ... and no "less restrictive means" ... are available to achieve the governmental interest.[53]

The Court agreed with the IRS. And Bob Jones University and its contributors lost their tax benefits.

While most Free Exercise cases challenge the government's right to prevent an individual from engaging in religious conduct, *Bowen v. Roy* (1986) challenged the government's right to engage in its own conduct detrimental to the individual's religious beliefs.[54]

Stephen Roy and Karen Miller applied for and began receiving welfare benefits from Pennsylvania, but they refused to provide their Social Security numbers. They also refused to apply for a Social Security number for their 2-year-old daughter, Little Bird of the Snow. Roy was a Native American, and he believed that using a number to identify his child would rob her of part of her spirit and keep her from getting greater spiritual power.

Since the federal government funded part of the welfare benefits, and because the federal government required Social Security numbers, Pennsylvania terminated some benefits and began proceedings to reduce others. Little Bird's parents then sued the U.S. Secretary of Health and Human Services, claiming that the federal law violated the First Amendment as applied to them.

Sometime during the trial the United States assigned Little Bird a Social Security number, but her parents did not use it. The District Court entered an injunction prohibiting the government from using Little Bird's Social Security number or denying her benefits based on her parents refusal to provide that number.

The Supreme Court justices could not agree on the standard for determining if Little Bird's parents had to provide her Social Security number before she could receive benefits. But eight justices did agree that the Free Exercise Clause does not prevent the government from using that number if it has it. As Chief Justice Burger stated for the Court:

> Never to our knowledge has the Court interpreted the First Amendment to require the Government *itself* to behave in ways that the individual believes will further his or her spiritual development or that of his or her family. The Free Exercise Clause simply cannot be understood to require the Government to conduct its own internal affairs in ways that comport with the religious beliefs of particular citizens. Just as the Government may not insist that appellees engage in any set form of religious observance, so appellees may not demand that the government join in their chosen religious practices by refraining from using a number to identify their daughter. "[T]he Free Exercise Clause is written in terms of what the government cannot do to the individual, not in terms of what the individual can extract from the government."[55]

Native Americans also attempted to dictate what the government could do in *Lyng v. Northwest Indian Cemetery Protective Association*.[56] The National Park Service wanted to build a road through part of a national forest that was next to the Hoopa Valley Indian Reservation. Although the Park Service wanted to build the road on public land, it would run close to some sites—also on public land—that were sacred to the Indians and used for meditation and other religious purposes. The Park Service had attempted to choose the least intrusive route, to limit the traffic noise, and to preserve the privacy of the sacred sites, but it could not fully satisfy the Native Americans without abandoning the road.

As in *Bowen*, the Court held in *Lyng* that the Free Exercise Clause does not require government to conform its own actions to someone else's religious beliefs. As a result, the government could use its land to build the road.

The Test Changes

Even though some of the Supreme Court's cases ruled in the Government's favor, all the cases that restricted an individual's actions found a compelling governmental interest. Then the Court decided *Employment Division v. Smith* (1990).[57]

Alfred Smith and Galen Black were members of the Native American Church, which used peyote, an illegal drug, during religious ceremonies. A nonprofit agency employed them as drug and alcohol abuse rehabilitation counselors, and the agency required its counselors to abstain from alcohol and illegal drugs. So when it discovered that Smith and Black had taken a small quantity of peyote during a religious ceremony, it fired them. Oregon then denied them unemployment benefits.

Since Smith and Black were fired for engaging in conduct required by their religion, they probably felt they were on solid ground challenging Oregon's denial of benefits. After all, *Sherbert*, *Thomas*, and *Hobbie* all held that a state could not make people choose between practicing their religion and collecting unemployment insurance.[58] Those cases did not involve illegal conduct, however. The majority of the Court thought this distinction was important.

The majority also concluded that the state did not even need a compelling interest to justify its actions. Although the opinion recognized that the Court had applied a compelling interest test in earlier unemployment compensation cases, it emphasized that the conduct involved in those cases (refusal to work on a person's sabbath) was not prohibited by state law. According to Justice Scalia, writing for the Court, "We have never held that an individual's religious beliefs excuse him from compliance with an otherwise valid law prohibiting conduct that the State is free to regulate."[59] The Court's opinion distinguished cases like *Cantwell* and *Yoder* because they involved other protections (freedom of speech, the right of parents to direct the education of their children) along with the Free Exercise Clause. It continued, "Although we have sometimes purported to apply the *Sherbert* test in contexts other than [unemployment compensation], we have always found the test satisfied."[60]

The Court found that the Free Exercise Clause did not prohibit Oregon from applying a generally applicable criminal law to religiously motivated conduct. And since it could apply that law to Smith and Black, it could also deny them unemployment benefits for violating it.

Justice O'Connor believed that Oregon had a compelling interest in banning peyote, even for religious reasons, because of the harm created by drug abuse. So she concurred in the end result. She did not join the majority opinion, however, because she could not agree with the majority's decision to disregard the compelling interest test. According to Justice O'Connor, the majority decision "dramatically departs from well-settled First Amendment jurisprudence, appears unnecessary to resolve the question presented, and is incompatible with our Nation's fundamental commitment to individual religious liberty."[61]

Like Justice O'Connor, Congress was not happy with the *Smith* decision. But what can Congress do if it disagrees with the Courts' interpretation of the Free Exercise Clause? Can it propose a constitutional amendment? Yes. Can it overrule the Supreme Court? No. Yet that is just what Congress tried to do. The next chapter discusses those events.

Question 1: In the late 1800s when the polygamy cases were decided, most Americans believed that Mormonism was an excuse for bigamy rather than a sincere religion. Since then, Mormonism has thrived (without polygamous marriages) and has become an established and respectable religion. If the Supreme Court decided the polygamy case today, do you think it would reach the same conclusion? Why or why not?

Question 2: Review the hypothetical case at the beginning of
Chapter 1 (The Discriminating Dress Code). If
the Cane County School Board tried to enforce its
dress code to prevent Cindy and Ben from wearing religious jewelry, would its action violate Cindy
and Ben's free exercise rights? Why or why not?

CHAPTER NINE
CONGRESS JOINS THE DEBATE

Religious groups were worried. What rights would governments trample now that the Supreme Court had done away with the compelling interest test? Would the Baptist majority in a dry town seek to prosecute Lutherans for using communion wine in a church within the town's borders? Would animal rights activists pressure state legislatures into adopting anticruelty laws that prohibited everyone—including Jewish rabbis—from killing animals by cutting their throats? *Employment Division v. Smith* seems to say that these restrictions would be perfectly acceptable under the Free Exercise Clause.[1]

The five justices who joined the Supreme Court's decision in *Smith* took a lonely stand. From conservative Christian groups to the ACLU, from Republicans to Democrats, from California to Indiana to New York, almost everyone was worried about the *Smith* decision.

Congress turned its worry into action.

The Religious Freedom Restoration Act of 1993[2]

The Religious Freedom Restoration Act of 1993 (RFRA) attempted to overturn *Smith* and readopt the compelling interest test. Under RFRA, a person claiming an exemption from a general law on religious grounds had to prove that the law was a substantial burden on his or her religious exercise. But if it was, the burden shifted to the government—federal, state, or local—to prove that it had a compelling interest and that the law was the least restrictive means of accomplishing that interest. If the government could not make that showing, it had to accommodate the religious behavior.

Smith was not the only case Congress wanted to overturn when it adopted RFRA. The Supreme Court had previously decided two other cases that rejected the compelling interest test when applied to prisons or the military.

In *O'Lone v. Estate of Shabazz* (1987), New Jersey prison officials prevented Islamic prisoners from attending Jumu'ah, a Muslim service held on Friday afternoons.[3] Inmates assigned to outside work details were not allowed to return to the prison to attend a service. Five members of the Court upheld the prison officials' actions, holding that "prison regulations alleged to infringe constitutional rights are judged under a 'reasonableness' test less restrictive than that ordinarily applied to alleged infringements of fundamental constitutional rights."[4]

The Court also applied a reasonableness test to military personnel in *Goldman v. Weinberger* (1986).[5] Simcha Goldman was an Orthodox Jew and an officer in the Air Force, where he served as a clinical psychologist. An Air Force regulation mandated uniform dress for Air Force personnel, but Goldman's superiors looked the other way when he wore his yarmulke in the mental health clinic or under his service cap. Then someone complained, and Goldman's superior officer felt compelled to enforce the dress regulation. Goldman sued to keep the Air Force from enforcing its regulation against him. But the Court deferred to the military authorities and determined that they had not violated Goldman's rights.

In spite of widespread outrage over the *Smith* decision and concerns with *O'Lone* and *Goldman*, it took Congress more than three years to pass RFRA because some members were afraid it would have unintended effects.[6] Some were concerned about how the law would affect cases involving abortion, funding for church-run social services and schools, and tax exemptions for religious organizations. RFRA's sponsors eventually satisfied those concerns by addressing them in either the legislation or the legislative history.

Other members were concerned that the compelling interest test would increase the number of prisoner-rights lawsuits and make it harder for prison officials to keep control. Senator Reid, a Democrat from Nevada, introduced an amendment to exempt prisons from the legislation, but the amendment did not pass. The sponsors of RFRA assured their fellow congressmen that safety and order in prisons is a compelling interest and that the courts would continue to give deference to prison officials in determining how best to achieve that goal. The compelling interest test would, however, require prison officials to accommodate prisoners' religious needs when practical.

The delay had nothing to do with the main purpose of that law. Congress agreed almost unanimously that *Smith* was wrong and Congress should do something about it. Once RFRA's sponsors addressed the concerns over other issues, it passed the Senate by 97 to 3 and passed the House by a large margin as well.

RFRA's legislative history—the House and Senate Committee reports and the floor debates—repeatedly states that Congress was not dictating how any particular case should turn out. The courts could still determine what met the compelling interest test based on the facts of each individual case. Congress merely wanted to turn the clock back before *Smith*.

Congress's attempt to overturn *Smith* was partially unsuccessful. In *City of Boerne v. Flores*, the Supreme Court invalidated those parts of the law that applied to state and local governments.[7]

Archbishop Flores filed suit against the city after its zoning board denied a building permit to enlarge a Catholic church located in a historic preservation district. Archbishop Flores claimed that the city's action violated RFRA because historic preservation was not a compelling governmental interest or, even if it was, the city's zoning law was not the least restrictive means of achieving that interest. The city defended its action by claiming that RFRA was unconstitutional. The Supreme Court agreed with the city and struck down RFRA.

City of Bourne was primarily a states' rights case. The Court ruled that the Fourteenth Amendment did not give Congress the authority to restrict the states' powers beyond the limits in the First Amendment. Since the Court has the ultimate authority to interpret the Constitution (a principle that was established in the 1803 case of *Marbury v. Madison*), and because the Court's decision in *Smith* had interpreted the First Amendment to allow the states to meet a lower standard than that imposed by RFRA, Congress did not have the power to apply RFRA to state and local governments.[8]

Congress had better success applying RFRA to federal action. In *Gonzales v. O Centro Espirita Beneficente Uniao Do Vegetal,* a case decided in February 2006, the Court affirmed a preliminary injunction prohibiting the Attorney General from enforcing the federal drug laws against a religious group for possessing a banned substance.[9] The group received communion by drinking a tea brewed from a plant containing a hallucinogenic substance covered by the Controlled Substances Act. In granting the preliminary injunction, the District Court held that the government had not shown the compelling interest required by RFRA. The Supreme Court agreed.

The Attorney General did not raise the First Amendment as a defense, probably because it would have been unsuccessful. Congress can modify any laws it has adopted as long as the modifications do not conflict with the U.S. Constitution. And since RFRA strengthens the free exercise rights imposed by the Constitution rather than weakening them, they do not conflict. The government did argue that Congress did not intend to modify the Controlled Substances Act when it adopted RFRA, but the Court held otherwise. So Congress did overturn some effects of *Smith*—although not the case itself—when federal action was involved.

The Religious Land Use and Institutionalized Persons Act of 2000[10]

Although *City of Bourne* made it clear that Congress could not overrule the Supreme Court or strip the states of their powers, that was not the end of the story for state and local governments. Congress responded to that case by enacting the Religious Land Use and Institutionalized Persons Act of 2000 (RLUIPA). The new law, however, was less sweeping than RFRA, dealing only with the two areas included in its title.

When the City of Bourne denied Archbishop Flores's application to enlarge the church, it hindered the Catholic Church's growth in that community. Other municipalities had also used land use ordinances to hinder growth or to eliminate religious bodies altogether. In the Congressional hearings, witnesses testified that one city refused to allow the Mormons to build a temple, purportedly because it was not in the community's aesthetic interests; that Orthodox Jews were denied the right to meet in a rented house within walking distance of their homes; and that some cities had effectively zoned new churches out of both residential and commercial areas. Since Congress believed that the ability to gather and worship together is at the core of religious freedom, RLUIPA required federal, state, and local governmental bodies to apply the compelling interest test to land use laws such as zoning and landmark ordinances and prohibited them from discriminating against religious groups in applying those ordinances.

The new law also required institutions—prisons, mental hospitals, and nursing homes, for example—to apply the compelling interest test in their dealings with institutionalized persons. Again, congressional testimony showed conduct that Congress considered abuses, including denying Jewish prisoners matzo (unleavened bread) during Passover even though Jewish organizations had offered to provide it free.

So why did Congress think RLUIPA would succeed where RFRA had failed? Because Congress based its authority on different sections of the Constitution. Congress had based RFRA on its authority under Section 5 of the Fourteenth Amendment to pass laws enforcing the states' obligations under that amendment. The problem was that the Supreme Court said in *Smith* that the states' free exercise obligation was only to meet a reasonableness test, not a compelling interest test, which meant RFRA expanded those obligations rather than just enforced them.

In contrast, Congress based RLUIPA primarily on the Spending and Commerce Clauses of the Constitution. With one exception, the land use restrictions only applied if the land use ordinance was part of a program or activity receiving financial assistance from the federal government, the burden on religion affected interstate commerce, or the ordinance required public officials to make individualized decisions in applying it. The new law also prohibited governments from discriminating against religious bodies. These last two provisions—applying RLUIPA to individualized decisions and forbidding discrimination—still relied on Section 5 of the Fourteenth Amendment but dealt with requirements that the Supreme Court had not changed in *Smith.*

Congress also based the safeguards for institutionalized persons on the Spending Clause and the Commerce Clause. These provisions applied only if the institution received federal financial assistance or if the burden on religion affected interstate commerce.

It did not take long before someone challenged the new law.

Cutter v. Wilkinson (2005)[11]
Ohio prison officials refused to accommodate certain religious practices from "nonmainstream" religions, banning religious reading materials and refusing to let inmates gather for group worship. Several inmates sued, claiming that Ohio's action violated the First and Fourteenth Amendments and RLUIPA. But Ohio claimed that RLUIPA violated the Establishment Clause.

This law survived the challenge. The Supreme Court unanimously held that RLUIPA fell within the "play in the joints" between the Establishment Clause and the Free Exercise Clause because it alleviated government-created burdens on private religious exercise. In other words, this was an area where Congress could choose to act—or choose not to act—without violating either clause. Therefore, the statute was constitutional and Congress could withdraw federal funding from state institutions that did not comply.

It is important to understand what this case did not say. The Court did not decide whether Ohio prison officials could outlaw the particular religious practices at issue without violating RLUIPA. The case was appealed before the state had an opportunity to show that it had a compelling governmental interest. If Ohio could prove that the religious reading material incited prisoners to violence and that prohibiting the material was the least restrictive means of preventing that violence, then Ohio could ban the reading material without losing its federal funding.

The case also did not directly address Congress's ability to adopt RLUIPA under the Spending Clause or the Commerce Clause. Although Ohio made those arguments earlier in the case, it did not raise them before the Supreme Court.

Finally, the Court did not say that prisons must go out of their way to accommodate inmates' harmless religious practices. The penalty for violating RLUIPA is the loss of a benefit (federal funding) that the federal government is not required to provide in the first place. Ohio could ignore RLUIPA if it is willing to fund its prisons without the federal government's help. The Court simply said that withdrawing federal funding did not violate the Establishment Clause.

In *Smith*, the Supreme Court appears to have eliminated the compelling interest test in most cases under the Free Exercise Clause. *Smith* distinguished cases that were coupled with other fundamental rights, such as freedom of speech, however. As discussed in the next chapter, even without Congressional interference the free speech cases still use the higher standard.

Question 1: Should Congress have tried to overturn the Supreme Court's decision in *Employment Division v. Smith* without amending the Constitution? Why or why not?

Question 2: Review the third hypothetical case in Chapter 1 (The Prison Bible Study). If Michael, David, Isaiah, and Emilio sued under RLUIPA, would the Court be likely to rule in their favor, or would it find that the prison has met the statute's compelling interest test? Why do you think it would reach this result?

CHAPTER TEN

YOU CAN'T SAY THAT HERE

The Italian movie *The Miracle* was the talk of New York City during the 1950 Christmas season. But it was not a mindless feel-good movie, and some Christians did not feel good about it.

The Miracle tells the story of a poor girl who meets a stranger she thinks is Saint Joseph. He gets her drunk, rapes her (off-screen), and disappears. When she discovers she is pregnant, she exclaims "it is the grace of God," runs into a nearby church, and prostrates herself before a statue of Saint Joseph. During her pregnancy, the village children torment the girl, and she becomes an outcast. When her labor pains begin, she flees to another church and gives birth in solitude. The movie ends as she gazes lovingly upon her new son.

nder New York law, films had to be licensed before they could be shown in movie theaters, and a license would not be issued if the film was "obscene, indecent, immoral, inhuman, sacrilegious," or likely to incite crime. So Joseph Burstyn, Inc., which owned the exclusive U.S. rights to distribute *The Miracle*, submitted it to the motion picture division of the New York education department. The movie made it by the censors, received a license, and began playing.

Then the New York Board of Regents began receiving complaints that the movie was sacrilegious. *The Miracle* received critical acclaim, and the Board of Regents also received letters—many from Christians—supporting the movie. After watching the film, however, the Board revoked its license, effectively removing it from the movie theaters.

The Supreme Court considered the Board of Regents' action and the validity of the New York law in *Joseph Burstyn, Inc. v. Wilson* (1952).[1] The Court found that "the state has no legitimate interest in protecting any or all religions from views distasteful to them which is sufficient to justify prior restraints upon the expression of those views. It is not the business of government in our nation to suppress real or imagined attacks upon a particular religious doctrine, whether they appear in publications, speeches, or motion pictures." [2] Therefore, banning sacrilegious speech violated the First Amendment, and *The Miracle* could return to movie theaters.

According to the First Amendment, "Congress shall make no law ... abridging the freedom of speech or of the press; or the right of the people peaceably to assemble, ..." Unlike the Establishment and Free Exercise Clauses, the Free Speech Clause is not limited to religion, and most free speech principles developed in different contexts. The same is true of the related freedoms of press and assembly. This chapter will explore the cases involving religion, but it will barely touch the surface of the free speech, press, and assembly rights granted by the First Amendment in other cases. That would be another book.

Unlike the Establishment and Free Exercise Clauses, the Free Speech Clause is not limited to religion

The Jehovah's Witnesses Lead the Way

In the religion context, the free speech challenges began with a string of Jehovah's Witness cases. Most of those cases arose from local restrictions on selling or distributing religious literature and soliciting contributions, and many of them sound the same.

The first Jehovah's Witness case was *Lovell v. City of Griffin* (1938).[3] Griffin convicted Alma Lovell of violating a city ordinance that required everyone who distributed literature within the city limits to obtain written permission first. Alma believed that Jehovah sent her to do his work, that handing out Jehovah's Witness literature was part of that work, and that applying for a permit was an act of disobedience. So she passed out free literature without a permit, and the city arrested, charged, and convicted her of violating the ordinance. Since she could not—or was not willing to—pay the $50 fine, she was sentenced to fifty days in jail.

The Supreme Court reversed Alma's conviction. It found the ordinance invalid on its face and condemned it for "strik[ing] at the very foundation of the freedom of the press by subjecting it to license and censorship."[4]

Schneider v. New Jersey (1939) involved house-to-house solicitation and distribution of literature and, as in *Lovell,* the city ordinance required a written permit.[5] Also as in *Lovell,* a Jehovah's Witness refused to obtain a permit and was arrested, charged, and convicted. The city said the ordinance protected its citizens from fraudulent solicitations, but the Court told it to find another way. According to the Court, the city could prosecute fraud after the fact, it could regulate commercial soliciting, and it could impose reasonable hours on other types of soliciting (including the religious soliciting done in this case), but it could not prevent Schneider from going house-to-house or require that she be preapproved to do so.

Watchtower Bible and Tract Society v. Village of Stratton is very similar.[6] The village adopted an ordinance prohibiting "canvassers" from going door-to-door without first obtaining a permit from the mayor's office. There was no charge for the permits and they were issued routinely, but the person applying for one was required to complete and sign a detailed registration form, to carry the permit, and to display it when requested. As in *Schneider,* the village claimed that the ordinance was necessary to prevent fraud by protecting residents from con artists, but a group of Jehovah's Witnesses claimed that it violated their First Amendment rights.

Eight justices agreed with the Jehovah's Witnesses and struck down the ordinance. As the opinion stated:

> It is offensive—not only to the values protected by the First Amendment, but to the very notion of a free society—that in the context of everyday public discourse a citizen must first inform the government of her desire to speak to her neighbors and then

> obtain a permit to do so. Even if the issuance of permits by the
> mayor's office is a ministerial task that is performed promptly and
> at no cost to the applicant, a law requiring a permit to engage in
> such speech constitutes a dramatic departure from our national
> heritage and constitutional tradition.[7]

What made this case so unusual is that it was decided in
2002—over fifty years after *Schneider* and other cases had seem-
ingly settled the issue.

Most of the Jehovah's Witness cases occurred in the 1940s.
Jamison v. Texas (1943) voided a Dallas ordinance prohibiting
handbill distribution on city streets; *Martin v. Struthers* (1943)
voided a Youngstown, Ohio, ordinance prohibiting handbill distribution door-to-door; *Jones v. City of Opelika* (1943) and *Follett
v. Town of McCormick* (1944) voided ordinances that prohibited
selling books door-to-door without buying a license; and *Saia v.
New York* (1948) voided a Lockport, New York, ordinance that
prohibited using loudspeakers without permission from the
police chief.[8] In these cases, the ordinance either absolutely
prohibited the conduct (regardless of time, place, or manner),
imposed a licensing tax, or gave a public official discretion to
allow or prohibit the activity.

The Supreme Court also voided a licensing ordinance in
Cantwell v. Connecticut (1940), which was discussed in Chapter 8
for its free exercise implications.[9] *Cantwell* involved more than
failure to obtain a permit, however, because Jesse Cantwell was
also convicted of a breach of the peace. His breach consisted
of stopping two men on a residential street, asking for and receiving the men's permission to play a record, and turning off
the record and leaving when the men told him they found it
offensive. The record attacked the Roman Catholic Church,
and the men happened to be Roman Catholics. But Jesse did
not threaten them and was, in fact, very courteous.

According to the Court, Jesse had not breached the peace
and the First Amendment protected his conduct. His actions
were only "an effort to persuade a willing listener to buy a book
or to contribute money in the interest of what Cantwell, however misguided others may think him, conceived to be true
religion."[10]

A breach-of-the-peace conviction met with a different result in *Chaplinsky v. New Hampshire* (1942).[11] Chaplinsky was distributing religious literature on the streets, and several people complained to the town marshal. Marshal Bowering knew that Chaplinsky's activities were lawful, and he said so to the people who complained. But he approached Chaplinsky, warned him that the crowd was getting restless, and left. Some time later there was a disturbance, and two things happened: Someone told Marshal Bowering that a riot was developing at the intersection where Chaplinsky had been distributing literature, and a traffic officer asked Chaplinsky to go to the police station with him. But that disturbance was not what got Chaplinsky arrested.

Chaplinsky's and Marshal Bowering's paths crossed between the intersection and the police station, and the marshal repeated his warning. Then Chaplinsky swore at him and called him a racketeer and a Fascist. So Marshal Bowering arrested Chaplinsky for violating an ordinance forbidding the use of offensive words or names addressed to someone in a public place with intent to offend him.

The Supreme Court upheld Chaplinsky's conviction. According to Justice Murphy writing for the Court:

> [I]t is well understood that the right of free speech is not absolute at all times and under all circumstances. There are certain well-defined and narrowly limited classes of speech, the prevention and punishment of which has never been thought to raise any Constitutional problem. These include the lewd and obscene, the profane, the libelous, and the insulting or "fighting" words — those which by their very utterance inflict injury or tend to incite an immediate breach of the peace. It has been well observed that such utterances are no essential part of any exposition of ideas, and are of such slight social value as a step to truth that any benefit that may be derived from them is clearly outweighed by the social interest in order and morality. "Resort to epithets or personal abuse is not in any proper sense communication of information or opinion safeguarded by the Constitution, and its punishment as a criminal act would raise no question under that instrument."[12]

The fact that Chaplinsky was engaging in religious conduct just before he uttered the offensive words did not save him.

The First Amendment only applies to governmental action—sometimes called "state action." After all, it says, "*Congress* shall make no law." And the Fourteenth Amendment, which applies the First to state and local governments, says "No *State* shall make or enforce any law." The line between government and private action is not always clear, however. In *Marsh v. Alabama* (1946), a Jehovah's Witness distributed literature on the sidewalk in Chickasaw's business district.[13] The district was close to and easily accessible from a main highway, served as a community shopping center, and was open to use by the public. Chickasaw resembled the surrounding communities in every way except one: It was a company-owned town.

The company had posted signs that identified the area as private property and stated that no one could solicit without written permission. Marsh was warned that she could not distribute her literature without permission and was told that she would not get permission. When she refused to leave, she was arrested and charged with a state crime for trespassing on private property.

Alabama denied that Marsh had free speech rights in a town owned by a private company rather than by a government. But the Court noted that Chickasaw had every other appearance of being public property, and the mere fact that it was owned by a private corporation was not enough to defeat Marsh's First Amendment claim. So Chickasaw had to open its streets to First Amendment activities.

In the more recent case of *Wooley v. Maynard* (1977), Mr. and Mrs. Maynard covered up the New Hampshire state motto—"Live Free or Die"—on their license plates because it was repugnant to their beliefs as Jehovah's Witnesses.[14] After being convicted three times of obscuring the motto and refusing to pay the fines that were imposed, Mr. Maynard served fifteen days in jail. Concerned that he would be prosecuted again, he and his wife filed a lawsuit to prevent New Hampshire from taking any further action against them.

Chief Justice Burger, writing for the Court, noted that "The right of freedom of thought protected by the First Amendment against state action includes both the right to speak freely and the right to refrain from speaking at all."[15] According to Burger:

> New Hampshire's statute in effect requires that appellees use their private property as a "mobile billboard" for the State's ideological message—or suffer a penalty, as Maynard already has. As a condition to driving an automobile—a virtual necessity for most Americans—the Maynards must display "Live Free or Die" to hundreds of people each day. The fact that most individuals agree with the thrust of New Hampshire's motto is not the test; ... The First Amendment protects the right of individuals to hold a point of view different from the majority and to refuse to foster, in the way New Hampshire commands, an idea they find morally objectionable.[16]

The Court also found that New Hampshire did not have a compelling interest in requiring the Maynards to display the state motto on their license plates. Therefore, the First Amendment allowed them to cover up the state motto without further prosecution.

Another group of Jehovah's Witness cases involved both the freedom to speak and the freedom to assemble. In *Cox v. New Hampshire* (1941), the Jehovah's Witnesses organized several groups to march in single file along the sidewalks of Manchester's business district.[17] Some of the marchers carried signs reading "Religion is a Snare and a Racket" on one side and "Serve God and Christ the King" on the other. Other signs and printed leaflets that the walkers handed to passersby invited the public to a speech later in the day.

The Witnesses did not apply for a permit, and the city arrested the marchers for violating a state statute giving cities authority to prohibit parades or processions unless the organizers obtained a special license. As interpreted by the New Hampshire Supreme Court, the statute allowed the city to regulate the time and place of parades so that the city could provide crowd control and minimize the disruption to other citizens going about their business, but it did not give the city discretion as to which groups could obtain a permit.

The Supreme Court upheld the statute. According to Chief Justice Hughes, writing for the Court, "If a municipality has authority to control the use of its public streets for parades or processions, as it undoubtedly has, it cannot be denied authority to give consideration, without unfair discrimination, to time, place, and manner in relation to the other proper uses of the streets. We find it impossible to say that the limited authority conferred by the licensing provisions of the statute in question as thus construed by the state court contravened any constitutional right."[18]

The New Hampshire statute also imposed a permit fee on any group receiving a special license. The fee was designed to recover the city's costs for police and any other city services it had to provide (for example, sweeping up any pamphlets thrown on the streets) but not to make money or discourage parades. So the Court upheld the fee as well.

The Jehovah's Witnesses had more success in two cases involving meetings in public parks. In *Niemotko v. Maryland* (1951), the Court reversed the disorderly conduct convictions of two speakers who held a Bible talk in a public park without a permit.[19] The speakers had applied for a permit but the city of Havre de Grace refused to grant one, apparently for no other reason than its dislike of the Witnesses. The meeting was orderly, and the two men went quietly when they were arrested. In other words, there was discrimination by the city and no disorder by the Witnesses.

Fowler v. Rhode Island involved a Pawtucket ordinance that prohibited political or religious meetings in its public parks.[20] The Jehovah's Witnesses held a religious meeting in Slater Park, and a visiting minister addressed the crowd of about 400 over two loudspeakers. The meeting was quiet and orderly, but the visiting minister was arrested anyway. Since the city allowed

Catholics and Protestants to hold religious services in city parks, its action against the Witnesses was clearly discriminatory. The Supreme Court could not tolerate that discrimination, and it reversed the minister's conviction.

Access to Public Facilities

Many of the Jehovah's Witness cases held that the public streets were public forums open to any type of speech. In *Jamison v. Texas,* for example, the Court rejected Dallas's claim that it could completely prohibit people from using the streets to communicate ideas. As Justice Black stated, "One who is rightfully on a street which the state has left open to the public carries with him there as elsewhere the constitutional right to express his views in an orderly fashion."[21]

So does the fact that something is a public forum mean there are no limitations at all on what someone can say or on how they can say it? No. In *Jamison,* Justice Black said people had a right to express their views "in an orderly fashion," and *Chaplinsky* upheld a conviction for using offensive words. Subsequent cases have further explained how governments can regulate speech in public forums.

Heffron v. International Society for Krishna Consciousness (1981)[22]
Followers of the Krishna religion wanted to sell religious literature and solicit contributions while walking around the grounds at the Minnesota State Fair. But the regulations governing the fair limited the distribution of literature and the solicitation of funds to fixed locations. Booths were available to anyone on a first-come, first-serve basis for a rental fee based on size and location. The regulations did not prohibit the Krishna or any other group from walking around and talking to people or from directing listeners to their booth; the only restriction was that they could not sell their literature or solicit contributions during the discussion.

The day before the 1977 Minnesota State Fair opened, the Krishna sued state officials and claimed that the regulations violated their First Amendment rights. In particular, the Krishna argued that Sankirtan, one of their religious rituals, required members to go into public places to distribute or sell religious literature and to solicit donations.

The Free Speech Clause does not provide an absolute right to speak at any time in any public place. The Court noted that governments can limit the time, place, and manner of speech as long as the restrictions serve an important government interest and are not based on either the content or the subject matter of the speech. Here, the regulation did not prohibit selling literature and soliciting contributions; it simply required that it be done from a fixed location. The regulation applied equally to everyone, so it did not discriminate against any particular content or subject matter. And, according to the Court, it served an important government interest by maintaining the orderly movement of the large crowds attending the fair. Therefore, the regulation was valid, and the Krishna could not sell their literature or solicit funds while walking among the crowd.

Airport Commissioners v. Jews for Jesus, Inc. (1987)[23]

Los Angeles airport officials adopted a resolution stating that "the Central Terminal Area of Los Angeles International Airport is not open for First Amendment activities by any individual and/or entity." Alan Snyder was distributing Jews for Jesus leaflets when an airport security officer stopped him. The security officer showed Alan a copy of the resolution, asked him to leave the airport, and said the city would take legal action if he continued to hand out the pamphlets. Alan left the airport and went to court.

Jews for Jesus first argued that the airport was a public forum and the resolution did not pass the test for limiting speech in that type of forum. The Court did not reach the question of whether an airport is a public forum, however. Instead, the Court unanimously struck down the ordinance because it was overbroad, banning every kind of First Amendment activity. It could even be read to prohibit passengers from talking to friends while waiting for an airplane.

International Society for Krishna Consciousness v. Lee (1992)[24]
Five years later, the Supreme Court was again asked to decide whether an airport is a public forum. This time the followers of the Krishna religion wanted to solicit contributions in the passenger terminals at the three major airports in the greater New York City area as part of their practice of Sankirtan. But the Port Authority of New York and New Jersey, which ran the three airports, prohibited selling or distributing literature or soliciting funds inside the terminal buildings. It did allow those activities on the sidewalks outside the terminals, however.

Chief Justice Rehnquist, writing for the Court, distinguished three types of forums and described the tests used to decide whether regulations limiting speech in each type were valid under the First Amendment.

> [R]egulation of speech on government property that has traditionally been available for public expression is subject to the highest scrutiny. Such regulations survive only if they are narrowly drawn to achieve a compelling state interest. The second category of public property is the designated public forum, whether of a limited or unlimited character—property that the State has opened for expressive activity by part or all of the public. Regulation of such property is subject to the same limitations as that governing a traditional public forum. Finally, there is all remaining public property. Limitations on expressive activity conducted on this last category of property must survive only a much more limited review. The challenged regulation need only be reasonable, as long as the regulation is not an effort to suppress the speaker's activity due to disagreement with the speaker's view.[25]

The Court found that airports are not places traditionally used for public speech and that the Port Authority had not opened up the terminals for speech by other groups. Therefore, the Court held that the Port Authority terminals were nonpublic forums. The Court also held that the regulation was a reasonable restriction considering that the persons solicited could be struggling with luggage or running for an airplane.

Capitol Square Review Board v. Pinette (1995)[26]

Ohio owned a plaza surrounding the Ohio Statehouse. Various groups used Capitol Square for speeches, rallies, and festivals. Although groups had to receive approval from the Capitol Square Review and Advisory Board before using the square, approval was almost automatic. A group merely had to fill out an application form and agree to a few conditions designed to ensure that the event was safe, sanitary, and did not interfere with other people using the square. There were no restrictions on the content of the message or the cause.

Over the years, a number of groups with widely different messages—from homosexual rights activists to the United Way to the Ku Klux Klan—had held rallies at Capitol Square. The square had also been the site of several unattended displays, including a Christmas tree, a privately placed menorah, and a display showing the progress of a United Way campaign.

In 1993, the Ohio chapter of the Ku Klux Klan filed an application to put up a cross in Capitol Square, and the board denied it. After trying unsuccessfully to get the decision reversed without going to court, the Ohio Klan's leader, Vincent Pinette, filed a lawsuit. The suit asked the district court to order the board to issue a permit allowing the Klan to put up the cross as an unattended display. The district court issued the order, and the board complied. The Sixth Circuit Court of Appeals and the Supreme Court affirmed the district court's order.

The Supreme Court noted that the Free Speech Clause requires governments to treat religious expression the same way it treats other expression. Since the board allowed other private groups to put up unattended displays involving nonreligious expression, it must allow the Klan to do the same with its religious expression.

The Supreme Court also rejected the board's defense that it would violate the Establishment Clause if it allowed the Klan to set up an unattended cross—a Christian symbol—so near the seat of government. The Court noted that Ohio did not sponsor the cross, the cross was on government property that had been opened to the public for similar use, and the Klan was required to go through the same application process and meet the same terms as other private groups. The Establishment Clause did not require the state to discriminate against religious expression under these circumstances.

Public Schools and Universities

The Court has generally treated public schools and universities as limited public forums. A number of cases have challenged regulations or practices denying religious groups access to public school facilities while granting access to other groups. And each of the educational bodies claimed, unsuccessfully, that providing access to the religious group would violate the Establishment Clause. Here are some of those cases.

Widmar v. Vincent (1981) [27]
From 1973 until 1977, a group of Christian students met regularly at the University of Missouri at Kansas City. Their organization, Cornerstone, registered with the university and routinely received permission to use its facilities as part of a stated policy to encourage the activities of student organizations.

Then the administration had a change of heart. The university had also adopted a regulation prohibiting the use of its facilities "for purposes of religious worship or religious teaching"—a regulation that had been in effect since 1972 but was not enforced, at least as to Cornerstone, until 1977. Then the administration told Cornerstone it could no longer meet in the university's building or grounds. Eleven students, all members of Cornerstone, sued.

The Court held that the university had violated the First Amendment by denying Cornerstone the right to meet in its facilities. According to the Court, the school's policy excluding religious groups while welcoming other student groups violated the Free Speech Clause because it was not content-neutral.

After noting that religious worship and discussion are forms of speech and association protected by the First Amendment, Justice Powell, writing for the Court, explained what the university would have to do to ban that speech.

> In order to justify discriminatory exclusion from a public forum
> based on the religious content of a group's intended speech, the
> University must therefore satisfy the standard of review appropriate
> to content-based exclusions. It must show that its regulation is
> necessary to serve a compelling state interest and that it is narrowly
> drawn to achieve that end.[28]

The university claimed that its desire to avoid violating the Establishment Clause gave it a compelling state interest. While the Court recognized that avoiding Establishment Clause violations might be a compelling interest, it did not agree that allowing religious groups to use the university's facilities on the same terms as other student groups would violate the Establishment Clause. Therefore, the university's regulation was invalid, and Cornerstone could continue meeting on its premises.

Lamb's Chapel v. Center Moriches School District (1993)[29]

The pastor of Lamb's Chapel wanted to use public school facilities to show a family values film series containing lectures by Dr. James Dobson. The school district had adopted a policy allowing community groups to use the school for social, civic, or recreational activities that were open to the public. The policy did not authorize meetings for religious purposes, so the school district denied the request.

The Supreme Court emphasized that schools do not have to allow other groups to use their facilities, either during or after school. They can choose to allow some uses but not others. They can make distinctions based on the subject matter. But they violate the First Amendment freedoms of speech and assembly if they authorize the use of their facilities and then make distinctions based on the group's views.

The line between subject matter and viewpoint is not always easy to find, however. The school district argued that its policy was viewpoint neutral because it did not allow any religious uses. Lamb's Chapel, on the other hand, argued that the subject was family values, and the religious orientation of the films was the viewpoint.

The Court agreed with Lamb's Chapel. The school district's policy allowed nonreligious community groups to use the school's facilities to disseminate information on family values, but it did not allow religious groups to do the same thing. Therefore, the school district's denial violated the Free Speech Clause unless the district could show a compelling interest.

As the university did in *Widmar*, the school district argued that its compelling interest was to avoid violating the Establishment Clause. And the school district had no better luck than the university. The Court noted that the film series would have been shown outside of school hours, would not have been sponsored by the school, would have been open to the public, and Lamb's Chapel would be just one of many private organizations to hold meetings on school premises. In these circumstances, there was little danger that anyone would think the school endorsed the views in the films. So the Establishment Clause did not prohibit Lamb's Chapel from showing the Dobson films.

Rosenberger v. University of Virginia (1995)[30]
Do monetary subsidies receive the same treatment as access to physical facilities? The University of Virginia established a category of independent student organizations called "contracted independent organizations" (CIOs). To qualify, these student groups were required to file their constitutions with the university, pledge not to discriminate in whom they admitted to membership, and include a disclaimer in their publications saying that they were independent organizations and that the university had no responsibility for them.

The university paid outside printers for the printing costs of CIOs' student publications. Wide Awake Productions, which students established to publish a student magazine with a Christian perspective, qualified as a CIO. When it asked the university to pay its printing costs, however, the university denied the request because the publication was a religious one.

The University of Virginia argued that this case was different from *Lamb's Chapel* because it involved monetary subsidies rather than the use of physical facilities. The Court did not see the importance of the distinction, however, so it held that the university had discriminated against Wide Awake Publications because of its religious viewpoint. And, as in previous cases, the Court rejected the university's Establishment Clause defense.

Good News Club v. Milford Central School (2001)[31]
Stephen and Darleen Fournier sponsored the local Good News Club, a private Christian organization for 6- to 12-year-olds. They wanted to hold weekly after-school club meetings in the school cafeteria. Milford's policy was very similar to the one in *Lamb's Chapel.* The policy said that district residents could use the school "for instruction in any branch of education, learning, or the arts" and for "social, civic, and recreational meetings and entertainment events" as long as the meetings were open to the public and approved by the school. The policy also prohibited use by any individual or organization for religious purposes.

The Fourniers submitted their request to the school, stating that the purpose of the club meetings was for "a fun time of singing songs, hearing a Bible lesson and memorizing scripture." The superintendent turned down the request under the religious use restriction, and Darlene Fournier asked the courts to intervene.

Consistent with earlier cases, the Supreme Court held that Milford's actions violated the club's free speech rights because it denied it the use of school facilities based on the club's religious viewpoint. The policy allowed activities that taught morals and character development to children and that is what the club wanted to do. According to the Court, if a school opens its doors to some groups to engage in those activities, it must open its doors to all groups wanting to do so.

Milford claimed that the religious nature of the club's activities made them different from other groups that taught morals and character development. The Court replied:

We disagree that something that is "quintessentially religious" or "decidedly religious in nature" cannot also be characterized properly as the teaching of morals and character development from a particular viewpoint ... . What matters for purposes of the Free Speech Clause is that we can see no logical difference in kind between the invocation of Christianity by the Club and the invocation of teamwork, loyalty, or patriotism by other associations to provide a foundation for their lessons.[32]

The Court then concluded that Milford had discriminated against the club on the basis of viewpoint and the restriction was not reasonable. The Court also rejected Milford's Establishment Clause defense.

Although a limited public forum cannot discriminate, it can restrict. Shortly after *Good News Club* was decided, news stories reported that the Milford Central School district was considering either banning all community groups from meeting at the school or closing it to community groups until 5:00 p.m.— long after the end of the school day. Rev. Stephen Fournier was quoted as saying that either approach would rule out club meetings at the school since the best opportunity to reach the children was right after school ended.[33]

The vast majority of the Free Speech Clause cases have prohibited governments from interfering with religious speech. The few cases decided against the speaker found that the activity involved nonreligious speech intended to offend (*Chaplinsky*),

> *The vast majority of the Free Speech Clause cases have prohibited governments from interfering with religious speech.*

the government did not ban all speech but simply placed reasonable restrictions on time or place (*Cox, Heffron*), or the speech took place in a nonpublic forum (*Lee*). The government has very limited authority to restrict religious speech.

Question 1: *The Good News Club* case implies that religious clubs designed to teach morals and character development must be treated the same as Boy Scouts, Girl Scouts, 4-H Clubs, and similar groups. A school district can, however, deny access to all those groups. As a practical matter, are Christians better off if religious clubs are discriminated against or if all character-building clubs are equally banned?

Question 2: Review the fourth hypothetical case (A Christmas Cross) from Chapter 1. Is the suburb violating the Harrises' free speech rights by fining them under the zoning ordinance? Why or why not?

CHAPTER ELEVEN
IT'S NONE OF OUR BUSINESS

The Civil War split churches as well as families. At the Walnut Street Presbyterian Church in Louisville, Kentucky, a majority of the church officers asked the voting members of the congregation to extend a call to a pastor who apparently supported slavery. When a majority of the voting members refused, the officers hired him anyway, and the rift between the two factions grew. Since the congregation was part of the Presbyterian Church in the United States (PCUS), a hierarchical body, it sent a committee to hold a congregational meeting and a new election.

The proslavery officers had the keys to the church and refused to open it for the congregational meeting, so the committee and the voting majority held the meeting on the sidewalk. Although they did not remove the existing officers, they elected enough additional officers to outvote the proslavery faction. Unfortunately for the majority, however, the officers refused to recognize the new election and claimed the church building for a different hierarchical body—one that had split off from PCUS when it took an antislavery, pro-Union stand.

The dispute lasted many years, and the war did not end the matter. It took a decision from the United States Supreme Court to return the church building to the antislavery majority.[1]

Who Decides?

Should the courts get involved in church disputes? According to the Supreme Court, the answer is both no and yes. The courts do not get involved in cases that revolve around doctrine, church governance, or other ecclesiastical issues. But they will get involved in property disputes and other matters that are similar to the secular issues courts are used to dealing with. After all, property rights are worthless if the courts will not enforce them.

Watson v. Jones (1871), the case involving the Walnut Street Church, illustrates the tension between these two concerns. As

Justice Miller explained in his opinion for the Court, it is reluctant to interfere in disputes within a religious body:

> The right to organize voluntary religious associations to assist in
> the expression and dissemination of any religious doctrine, and
> to create tribunals for the decision of controverted questions of
> faith within the association, and for the ecclesiastical government
> of all the individual members, congregations, and officers within
> the general association, is unquestioned. All who unite themselves
> to such a body do so with an implied consent to this government,
> and are bound to submit to it. But it would be a vain consent and
> would lead to the total subversion of such religious bodies, if any
> one aggrieved by one of their decisions could appeal to the secular
> courts and have them reversed. It is of the essence of these religious
> unions, and of their right to establish tribunals for the decision of
> questions arising among themselves, that those decisions should
> be binding in all cases of ecclesiastical cognizance, subject only to
> such appeals as the organism itself provides for.[2]

Nonetheless, the Court recognized that it must be able to decide civil rights that a church has refused to acknowledge or found itself unable to protect. The property laws are civil laws, and the civil courts must be able to enforce them.

That does not mean that courts can ignore church decisions in deciding civil disputes. Many civil disputes are resolved by looking at what the parties expected before the dispute arose. Did the church body expect church property to belong to the officers? To the majority within the congregation? To the hierarchical body? And how does a court decide what the parties expected?

Watson said that disputes over property held for religious purposes fall into three categories. If a donor gave the property to the religious organization by a deed or a will, the terms of the deed or will may dictate who owns the property or what purposes the organization can use it for. If the property is held by an independent religious group, such as a church with a congregational governing structure, the group's rules of government will apply—if a church's constitution says the majority rules, then the majority wins. If the property is held by a group that belongs to a hierarchical religious organization, like PCUS, courts will normally defer to the hierarchical body.

The Court followed this principle in Watson. PCUS gave its blessing to the second election, which gave control to the loyal majority. So the Court did, too.

The Supreme Court has decided a handful of other cases involving internal church disputes. It has consistently declined to decide questions involving religious doctrine or qualifications but has allowed states to apply neutral principles to property disputes. Here are those cases.

Smith v. Swormstedt (1853)[3]

The Methodist Episcopal Church knew it would split if the country did, and it wanted the split to be friendly. So it worked out a plan for separation that was approved by over three-fourths of the voting members of the General Conference, its highest body. The plan allowed the Southern churches to decide whether to divide the church body into the Methodist Episcopal Church North and the Methodist Episcopal Church South. Once they voted to do so, the property held by the old denomination was to be divided proportionately to the number of ministers in each new denomination.

Among that property was the Book Concern, a religious publishing company started by the ministers themselves and eventually transferred to the Methodist Episcopal Church in trust for its ministers and their families. The Book Concern started from modest roots but become a very profitable operation with significant holdings.

At first, the plan for division seemed to work. The Southern churches voted to divide, and the ME Church South apparently received much of the property it was entitled to under the agreement. In fact, the Court noted that the Northern bishops all regarded the plan as binding. But the trustees for the

Book Concern felt different and were unwilling to give the ME Church South its share. So the Supreme Court had to step in.

Although it would be more than a decade before the Court decided *Watson*, its decision was consistent with that case. The Court accepted the action of the hierarchical body and validated the agreement adopted by the General Conference. As a result, the trustees of the Book Concern were required to transfer a proportionate share—approximately one-third—to trustees chosen by the ME Church South to be used for the same purpose as the original trust.

Bouldin v. Alexander (1872)[4]
One year after it decided *Watson*, the Court was confronted with a dispute in a church with a congregational governing structure. A minority from the Third Colored Baptist Church of Philadelphia tried to become the majority by excommunicating everyone who disagreed with them. The Court invalidated the minority's actions, and Justice Strong explained the Court's reasoning as follows:

> This is not a question of membership of the church, nor of the rights of members as such. It may be conceded that we have no power to revise or question ordinary acts of church discipline, or of excision from membership … . But we may inquire whether the resolution of expulsion was the act of the church, or of persons who were not the church and who consequently had no right to excommunicate others. And, thus inquiring, we hold that the action of the small minority, on the 7th and 10th of June, 1867, by which the old trustees were attempted to be removed, and by which a large number of the church members were attempted to be exscinded, was not the action of the church, and that it was wholly inoperative. In a congregational church, the majority, if they adhere to the organization and to the doctrines, represent the church. An expulsion of the majority by a minority is a void act.[5]

Although it appears on first glance that the Court got involved in the church's internal functioning, the Court stayed true to the principles it had announced in *Watson*. By voiding the actions of the minority, it affirmed the power of the majority to govern an independent church.

Shepard v. Barkley (1918)[6]

PCUS merged with the Cumberland Presbyterian Church, which was composed of congregations that had previously left PCUS because of doctrinal disagreements. After PCUS adopted changes to its doctrine, both denominations held General Assemblies and voted to merge. A vocal minority from the now former Cumberland Presbyterian Church objected and claimed that the denomination still existed and continued to own churches and a local college.[7]

The district court held that the dispute was really one of doctrine, that the highest governing body of each denomination had determined that the differences in doctrine were now insignificant and had voted to merge, and that the courts would not second-guess the decisions made by those hierarchical church bodies. It then held that the churches and the college belonged to the merged PCUS, and the Eighth Circuit Court of Appeals agreed. When the case reached the Supreme Court, it affirmed in a very short opinion, simply stating that the principles in *Watson* were so well-settled that there was no need to discuss them again.

Gonzalez v. Roman Catholic Archbishop of Manila (1929)[8]

Raul Gonzalez wanted to be a chaplain in the Roman Catholic Archdiocese of Manila. Or, more accurately, he wanted the money the chaplain would receive. Unfortunately for Raul, he had two problems. He was only ten years old, and he was not qualified under the church's laws.

The case had its roots back in the days when a layperson could fund a Roman Catholic chaplaincy and dictate who would fill it. This particular chaplaincy was created in 1820 and funded with property left to the archdiocese in the donor's will. The will said it should go to her great-grandson, and then to the nearest relative, and be passed down to her descendants. If there were no descendants available to fill the position, the archdiocese could give it to someone from the local college.

By 1922, the great-grandson and four other descendants had held the chaplaincy. But it had been empty since 1910, when Raul's father resigned to get married. Over the years, the modest income from the property had swelled to a large one, and Raul—or perhaps his father—wanted that income. So he asked the archbishop to appoint him to the chaplaincy and to pay him the income for the entire time the position had been vacant. Not surprisingly, the archbishop refused.

Since the Philippines was a United States territory at the time, the case eventually ended up before the Supreme Court. The Court first looked at the terms of the will and determined that the donor intended that the chaplaincy be held by someone who was qualified to serve under the rules of the Roman Catholic Church in effect at the time of each individual appointment. It then looked at the church's current rules and determined that they required a chaplain to study for the priesthood at an approved seminary. The Court agreed with the archbishop that Raul did not meet those qualifications, and it denied Raul both the appointment and the income.

Although the Court agreed with the archbishop, it did look at the Roman Catholic laws along the way. It also suggested, in passing, that fraud, collusion, or arbitrariness might be grounds for disregarding the church's decisions on ecclesiastical matters when they affect nonecclesiastical rights. Finally, it held that the courts had jurisdiction to hear the case because Raul claimed, in substance, that he was the beneficiary of a trust, and the courts are responsible for enforcing trusts.

Kedroff v. St. Nicholas Cathedral (1952)[9]

The Cold War was raging, and anything Russian was suspect. New York passed a law transferring control of the North American branch of the Russian Orthodox Church from the hierarchical church authorities in Moscow to authorities selected by a convention of North American churches. Archbishop Fedchenkoff, who was appointed by the authorities in Russia, refused to recognize the transfer and would not vacate the Russian Orthodox cathedral in New York City. The "new" church authorities, selected at the convention, then sued for possession.

The Supreme Court sided with Archbishop Fedchenkoff and the authorities in Moscow. According to the Court, "Legislation that regulates church administration, the operation of the churches, the appointment of clergy" violates the church's free exercise rights.[10] The Court went on to say that transferring control over churches by statute "violates our rule of separation between church and state."[11] The law was invalid, and the Moscow authorities retained control over the cathedral.

Kreshik v. St. Nicholas Cathedral (1960)[12]

New York did not give up that easily. Although the U.S. Supreme Court struck down the legislature's attempts to separate the Russian Orthodox Church from its roots, the New York Court of Appeals decided it could reach the same result without the statute. It found that the secular government in the U.S.S.R. dominated the head of the Russian Orthodox Church in Moscow and, therefore, that New York common law (in other words, law developed by the courts over the years) prohibited him from exercising any control over the cathedral.

> *... courts have no more right to interfere in a church's internal affairs than legislatures do.*

The U.S. Supreme Court again sided with the authorities in Moscow. In a very short opinion, it held that courts have no more right to interfere in a church's internal affairs than legislatures do.

Presbyterian Church v. Hull Church (1969)[13]

By 1969, the *Watson* principles were starting to crumble, at least when property ownership was the issue. PCUS was again at the heart of the controversy. This time there was dissension among the churches in Georgia, and two local churches withdrew from the larger church body. Instead of taking their property dispute to the PCUS General Assembly, they filed in Georgia state court.

The Georgia judge applied state trust law and instructed the jury that who owned the property depended on whether PCUS had changed its doctrine since the local churches affiliated with it. The jury found that it had, so the state court held that the individual congregations owned the property, and the Georgia Supreme Court agreed.

The U.S. Supreme Court reversed, holding that the Georgia courts violated the First Amendment by looking at church doctrine. But it left the door open for courts to resolve church property disputes on more neutral grounds. Writing for the Court, Justice Brennan stated:

> Thus, the First Amendment severely circumscribes the role that civil courts may play in resolving church property disputes. It is obvious, however, that not every civil court decision as to property claimed by a religious organization jeopardizes values protected by the First Amendment. Civil courts do not inhibit free exercise of religion merely by opening their doors to disputes involving church property. And there are neutral principles of law, developed for use in all property disputes, which can be applied without "establishing" churches to which property is awarded. But First Amendment values are plainly jeopardized when church property litigation is made to turn on the resolution by civil courts of controversies over religious doctrine and practice.[14]

Maryland & Virginia Eldership of the Church of God v. Church of God at Sharpsburg, Inc. (1970)[15]

Maryland walked through the neutral principles door in one of the few cases that did not involve PCUS. When two congregations seceded from the Church of God, the Maryland courts looked at the deeds, the churches' charters, and provisions in the Church of God constitution regarding property ownership. The courts then awarded the property to the individual congregations. In a one-paragraph decision, the Supreme Court dismissed the appeal because the courts did not base their decision on religious doctrine. So the state courts' decision stood.

Serbian Eastern Orthodox Diocese v. Milivojevich (1976)[16]

The higher church authorities in the Serbian Eastern Orthodox Church appointed Bishop Milivojevich as head of the Church's American-Canadian Diocese. But after twenty or more years in that role, he wanted more autonomy for the diocese. And so began a long struggle for control between Bishop Milivojevich and the church authorities in Serbia. Eventually the chasm became so wide that the higher church authorities reorganized the North American branch of the church and defrocked Bishop Milivojevich. He and his followers separated from the international church, declaring that the American-Canadian Diocese was no longer subject to the authorities in Serbia.

Then the battle moved to the Illinois courts. Since the head of the diocese technically owned the diocese's properties, the primary question was whether Bishop Milivojevich or the Serbian Church's more recent appointee was head of the diocese. Seizing on the arbitrariness exception suggested by *Gonzalez,* the Illinois Supreme Court ruled that the Serbian proceedings to reorganize the church in America and to defrock the bishop did not comply with the Church's internal rules so they were arbitrary and invalid. As a result, the Illinois court gave control of the diocese and its property and assets to Milivojevich and his followers.

Bishop Milivojevich's victory was short-lived, however. Justice Brennan wrote the opinion for the Court and held that the state court action violated the First Amendment. In this case, the Illinois Supreme Court's decision was unconstitutional because "it rests upon an impermissible rejection of the decisions of the highest ecclesiastical tribunals of this hierarchical church upon the issues in dispute, and impermissibly substitutes its own inquiry into church polity and resolutions ... ."[17] The opinion also clarified that there is no room for an arbitrariness exception where doctrine is involved. "[I]t is the essence of religious faith that ecclesiastical decisions are reached and are to be accepted as matters of faith whether or not rational or measurable by objective criteria."[18] The Court then concluded:

In short, the First and Fourteenth Amendments permit hierarchical religious organizations to establish their own rules and regulations for internal discipline and government, and to create tribunals for adjudicating disputes over these matters. When this choice is exercised and ecclesiastical tribunals are created to decide disputes over the government and direction of subordinate bodies, the Constitution requires that civil courts accept their decisions as binding upon them.[19]

The Serbian church officials prevailed, and Bishop Milivojevich lost his control over the diocese and its property.

Jones v. Wolf (1979)[20]

Milivojevich did not end the courts' involvement in church property disputes, however. Once again, the PCUS had dissension in its ranks. The members of the Vineville Presbyterian Church voted 164 to 94 to leave the PCUS and affiliate with another established Presbyterian denomination. The PCUS appointed a commission to resolve the disagreement, if possible, but the majority did not cooperate and the effort failed. The commission then ruled that the minority faction was the true congregation of the Vineville Presbyterian Church. The majority did not appeal the ruling to a higher authority within the PCUS.

Since the majority had possession of the church building, the minority sued to establish its ownership. The Georgia courts gave title to the majority, however, claiming that they were applying the "neutral principles of law" approach the Court appeared to endorse in *Hull Church*. The state courts looked at the deed (which conveyed the property to the local church) and at the PCUS constitution and governing documents (which were apparently silent about the ownership of congregational property).

This time the Supreme Court addressed the neutral principles approach head-on and gave it its blessing. Justice Blackmun's opinion for the Court stated:

> The primary advantages of the neutral-principles approach are that it is completely secular in operation, and yet flexible enough to accommodate all forms of religious organization and polity. The method relies exclusively on objective, well-established concepts of trust and property law familiar to lawyers and judges. It thereby promises to free civil courts completely from entanglement in questions of religious doctrine, polity, and practice.[21]

Justice Blackmun went on to note that any church body can determine who gets the property simply by putting it in its constitution or in the individual property deeds.

The Court was not sure what the Georgia Supreme Court based its decision on, however, so it remanded the case and asked the Georgia Supreme Court to determine whether the state courts had applied neutral principles of law. The Georgia Supreme Court answered the question in the affirmative, and this time the U.S. Supreme Court refused to hear it. So the majority got to keep the church property.

The cases leave some important questions unanswered. Since each case depends on its facts, they provide little real guidance for drawing the line between those situations—such as *Milivojevich*—where a property dispute involves church doctrine and internal government and those situations—such as *Jones*—where it does not. And can courts use "neutral principles of law" that apply only to churches, or must they apply rules used in similar disputes between other types of parties?

Fortunately, cases involving internal church disputes are rare. And when the courts intervene, they do so reluctantly. The Court held off deciding *Watson* for a year, hoping that, since the Civil War had ended, "that charity, which is so large an element in the faith of both parties, and which, by one of the apostles of that religion, is said to be the greatest of all the Christian virtues, would have brought about a reconciliation.

But we have been disappointed."[22] The Court felt it had no other choice than to decide the case. But it would rather have said, "it's none of our business."

Question 1: Should the courts intervene in disputes within independent congregations where the two factions disagree on whether the election of officers was valid? Does your answer change if the dispute is over which minister to call? If you do not believe the courts should get involved, how can the dissenting faction make sure its rights are protected?

Question 2: Assume that a local church constitution says the church and its property belong to those members who will continue its affiliation with a particular hierarchical body. The church constitution also says, however, that it will belong to the heirarchical body only as long as that body accepts certain creeds. If a majority of the members of the congregation believe the hierarchical body is departing from the substance of the creeds while continuing to give them lip service, should the courts defer to the hierarchical body's statement that it accepts the creeds and award the property to the members who remain loyal to that body?

CHAPTER TWELVE
THE ANSWER?

Alexis de Tocqueville visited the United States from France in 1831. During the visit, he asked several priests why religion was such a powerful force in American life, and "they all attributed the peaceful dominion of religion in their country mainly to the separation of church and state."[1] Tocqueville continued, "I do not hesitate to affirm that during my stay in America I did not meet with a single individual, of the clergy or of the laity, who was not of the same opinion on this point."[2] Based on his experience, de Tocqueville reached the following conclusion:

"In America religion is perhaps less powerful than it has been at certain periods and among certain nations; but its influence is more lasting. It restricts itself to its own resources, but of these none can deprive it: its circle is limited, but it pervades it and holds it under undisputed control."[3]

ould the founding fathers have been pleased with de Tocqueville's observations? What would they have thought about the Supreme Court's decisions interpreting the First Amendment? Both questions may be unanswerable. Nor can anyone predict with certainty how the Court will rule on any future case. Still, its previous decisions do provide some clues. Following are my educated guesses on what the Court would do with the hypothetical cases described at the beginning of this book.

Hypothetical Case 1: The Discriminating Dress Code

After one high school gang started wearing a particular type of cross to identify its members, the Cane County School Board banned religious symbols on clothing and jewelry. But Cindy wears a cross necklace as a witness to her Christian beliefs, and Ben wears a Star of David lapel pin as a symbol of his Jewish faith. If these students challenged the dress code under the First Amendment, what would the courts decide?

The Establishment Clause may be the weakest ground for challenging the school's actions. *Lemon v. Kurtzman* said that a law (or, in this case, a dress code) may violate the Establishment Clause if its principal effect is to either advance or inhibit religion.[4] But the Supreme Court's Establishment Clause cases involved situations that someone claimed advanced religion, not situations they claimed inhibited it.

Cindy and Ben might have better success under the Free Exercise Clause, but even that result is unclear. *Employment Division v. Smith* said that a governmental body can apply a law of general applicability to religious conduct if there is a valid reason for the law.[5] Preventing gang identification and violence is certainly a valid reason. But is the dress code a law of general applicability? On the one hand, it applies equally to all students and is aimed at gangs, not religious groups, but on the other it singles out religious symbols. Even if it is not a law of general applicability, however, the courts might find that the school's need to prevent gang violence meets the compelling interest test. The question is too close to call.

The success of a free exercise claim may also partly rest on whether the students believe that their religions require them to wear religious symbols. *Braunfeld v. Brown* held that the Free Exercise Clause does not require the state to accommodate voluntary religious behavior, although *Frazee v. Illinois* says it is what the individual believes his or her religion requires, rather than what the religious leaders say it requires, that counts.[6]

Cindy and Ben's best argument is that the dress code violates their free speech rights. When they wear their religious jewelry, they are making a statement about their religious beliefs. And the dress code is not content neutral because it singles out religious speech. Therefore, the dress code, as written, is probably unconstitutional.

If the school board were to revise the dress code to prohibit all symbols, that would create a closer question. Cindy and Ben would have to show that it violates their free speech rights as applied to them. Then the school would have to prove that it has a compelling interest to apply it to all symbols, including the religious ones these two students wear. The Court might, however, find a compelling interest because of the difficulty school officials would face in determining who wore the symbols for religious reasons and who wore them for gang identification.

Hypothetical Case 2: A Town with Heart

Milton Jones dies and leaves money to his hometown to erect a statue of Mother Theresa in the town square as a reminder that the town stands for "loving our neighbors, helping the poor, and having an open heart." The town board agrees to the terms of the bequest, but a small group of citizens claims that a statue of a religious person would violate the Establishment Clause.

The town is likely to win this case. The statue passes the purpose test since the bequest states a secular purpose and there is no reason to question that purpose. It probably also passes the endorsement test since a statue of a religious person is not likely, by itself, to tell the community that the town is supporting Christianity—especially since many people think of Mother Theresa as a humanitarian rather than as a Christian. *Van Orden v. Perry* says that context is important, however.[7] If the square includes secular statues or memorials, adding a statue of Mother Theresa should pass the endorsement test. If she is the only one there and the town surrounds her statue with candles and flowers and turns it into a religious shrine, it probably will not.

Hypothetical Case 3: The Prison Bible Study

Michael, David, Isaiah, and Emilio are Adams Correctional Center inmates who want to meet in a cell and hold a Bible study during the evening recreation period. Prison officials deny the request because inmates meeting in small groups could conspire against them, plan a prison break, or create gang loyalty. The prisoners claim that the denial violates their rights under the Free Exercise Clause.

The inmates would probably lose their First Amendment claim. *O'Lone v. Estate of Shabazz* said that prison regulations can impose burdens on religious conduct if they are reasonably related to the prison's needs.[8] Prohibiting small group meetings to keep order—and inmates—in the prison certainly meets this test.

The prison's action may, however, violate the Religious Land Use and Institutionalized Persons Act of 2000. That law prohibits prison officials from interfering with inmates' free exercise rights unless they have a compelling governmental interest, and the Court upheld that part of the law in *Cutter v. Wilkinson*.[9] Whether the government meets this stricter test under the facts in the hypothetical case is a close question and could go either way. If prison officials could not meet the test, they would have to accommodate the Bible study request (even if it cost them extra money to pay a guard to patrol the cell area) or lose their federal funding.

Hypothetical Case 4: A Christmas Cross

Bob and Karen Harris want to remind their neighbors that Christmas is all about Christ, but their 4-foot manger scene goes unnoticed because they live between two houses that cram their yards full of Santas, reindeer, snowmen, and other secular symbols. So they make their display more prominent by adding a lighted, 8-foot wooden cross behind the manger scene. Unfortunately, the cross violates the suburb's residential zoning ordinance, which prohibits freestanding figures higher than four feet. The suburb fines Bob and Karen for violating the ordinance, and they challenge the fine under the Free Speech Clause.

Bob and Karen would probably win their case. The cross is clearly nonverbal speech because Bob and Karen are using it to send a message—that Christmas is all about Christ. The suburb has no more of a compelling interest in regulating the height of freestanding figures than New Hampshire had of mandating the motto on its license plates in *Wooley v. Maynard*; and *Employment Division v. Smith* recognized that the compelling interest test still applies to free speech cases.[10] If the suburb's interest is in aesthetics, then that is clearly not a compelling interest. And if its interest is in safety—from a fear that the high winds in the area could knock over or break a taller display and injure someone in the process—the suburb can satisfy that interest by adopting structural requirements rather than height restrictions. So the suburb probably cannot apply the ordinance to Bob and Karen's cross.

The conservative justices tend to interpret both religion clauses narrowly. With the conservative justices leading the way, the Court said the Establishment Clause does not prohibit a public school district from paying for a sign language interpreter for a student attending a Catholic high school (*Zobrest v. Catalina Foothills School District*) or a state from giving poor children tuition vouchers usable at any school in the state, including a parochial school (*Zelman v. Simmons-Harris*).[11] And it said the Free Exercise Clause does not protect Native Americans who use a small amount of peyote in their religious ceremonies (*Employment Division v. Smith*), Muslim prisoners who are denied the right to attend Friday afternoon services (*O'Lone v. Estate of Shabazz*), or Orthodox Jews who violate Air Force regulations by wearing yarmulkes while on duty (*Goldman v. Weinberger*).[12]

In contrast, the liberal justices tend to interpret both clauses broadly. With the liberal justices voting with the majority, the Court has interpreted the Establishment Clause to prohibit states from requiring biology teachers to teach creation science along with evolution (*Edwards v. Aguillard*) and to remove state-sponsored prayers from public school graduations and football games (*Lee v. Weisman* and *Santa Fe v. Doe*).[13] The liberal justices have not voted with the majority in a Free Exercise case

The conservative justices treat religion as just another activity, while the liberal justices treat it as something sacred (which means "set apart" or "worthy of respect").

for decades, but they voted to interpret that Clause broadly to allow the conduct the Court prohibited in *Smith*, *O'Lone*, and *Goldman*.

The result is ironic. The conservative justices treat religion as just another activity, while the liberal justices treat it as something sacred (which means "set apart" or "worthy of respect").[14]

Regardless of the outcome of individual cases, justices from both sides of the aisle appear to agree with the following statement by Justice Jackson, writing in dissent in *Everson v. Board of Education*.

> [W]e cannot have it both ways. Religious teaching cannot be a private affair when the state seeks to impose regulations which infringe on it indirectly, and a public affair when it comes to taxing citizens of one faith to aid another, or those of no faith to aid all. … If the state may aid these religious schools, it may therefore regulate them.[15]

The conservatives choose to aid and regulate religion, while the liberals choose to do neither. Which result is better for Christianity and other organized religions? You decide.

Question 1: Grade the Supreme Court on how correctly is it interpreting the First Amendment. What is the grade based on?

Question 2: Has your opinion changed since reading this book? If so, how?

APPENDIX A[1]
SATURDAY, AUGUST 15, 1789
AMENDMENTS TO THE CONSTITUTION.

The House again went into a Committee of the whole on the proposed amendments to the constitution, Mr. BOUDINOT in the chair.

The fourth proposition being under consideration, as follows:

Article 1. Section 9. Between paragraphs two and three insert "no religion shall be established by law, nor shall the equal rights of conscience be infringed."

Mr. SYLVESTER had some doubts of the propriety of the mode of expression used in this paragraph. He apprehended that it was liable to a construction different from what had been made by the committee. He feared it might be thought to have a tendency to abolish religion altogether.

Mr. VINING suggested the propriety of transposing the two members of the sentence.

Mr. GERRY said it would read better if it was, that no religious doctrine shall be established by law.

Mr. SHERMAN thought the amendment altogether unnecessary, inasmuch as Congress had no authority whatever delegated to them by the constitution to make religious establishments; he would, therefore, move to have it struck out.

Mr. CARROLL.—As the rights of conscience are, in their nature, of peculiar delicacy, and will little bear the gentlest touch of governmental hand; and as many sects have concurred in opinion that they are not well secured under the present constitution, he said he was much in favor of adopting the words. He thought it would tend more towards conciliating the minds of the people to the Government than almost any other amendment he had heard proposed. He would not contend with gentlemen about the phraseology, his object was to secure the substance in such a manner as to satisfy the wishes of the honest part of the community.

Mr. MADISON said, he apprehended the meaning of the words to be, that Congress should not establish a religion, and enforce the legal observation of it by law, nor compel men to worship God in any manner contrary to their conscience. Whether the words are necessary or not, he did not mean to say, but they had been required by some of the State Conventions, who seemed to entertain an opinion that under the clause of the constitution, which gave power to Congress to make all laws necessary and proper to carry into execution the constitution, and the laws made under it, enabled them to make laws of such a nature as might infringe the rights of conscience, and establish a national religion; to prevent these effects he presumed the amendment was intended, and he thought it as well expressed as the nature of the language would admit.

Mr. HUNTINGTON said that he feared, with the gentleman first up on this subject, that the words might be taken in such latitude as to be extremely hurtful to the cause of religion. He understood the amendment to mean what had been expressed by the gentleman from Virginia; but others might find it convenient to put another construction upon it. The ministers of their congregations to the Eastward were maintained by the contributions of those who belonged to their society; the expense of building meeting-houses was contributed in the same manner. These things were regulated by bylaws. If an action was brought before a Federal Court on any of these cases, the person who had neglected to perform his engagements could not be compelled to do it; for a support of ministers, or building of places of worship might be construed into a religious establishment.

By the charter of Rhode Island, no religion could be established by law; he could give a history of the effects of such a regulation; indeed the people were now enjoying the blessed fruits of it. He hoped, therefore, the amendment would be made in such a way as to secure the rights of conscience, and a free exercise of the rights of religion, but not to patronize those who professed no religion at all.

Mr. MADISON thought, if the word national was inserted before religion, it would satisfy the minds of honorable gentlemen. He believed that the people feared one sect might obtain a pre-eminence, or two combine together, and establish a religion to which they would compel others to conform. He thought if the word national was introduced, it would point the amendment directly to the object it was intended to prevent.

Mr. LIVERMORE was not satisfied with that amendment; but he did not wish them to dwell long on the subject. He though it would be better if it was altered, and made to read in this manner, that Congress shall make no laws touching religion, or infringing the rights of conscience.

Mr. GERRY did not like the term national, proposed by the gentlemen from Virginia, and he hoped it would not be adopted by the House. It brought to his mind some observations that had taken place in the conventions at the time they were considering the present constitution. It had been insisted upon by those who were called antifederalists, that this form of Government consolidated the Union; the honorable gentleman's motion shows that he considers it in the same light. Those who were called antifederalists at that time complained that they had injustice done them by the title, because they were in favor of a Federal Government, and the others were in favor of a national one; the federalists were for ratifying the constitution as it stood, and the others not until amendments were made. Their names then ought not to have been distinguished by federalists and antifederalists, but rats and antirats.

Mr. MADISON withdrew his motion, but observed that the words "no national religion shall be established by law," did not imply that the Government was a national one; the question was then taken on Mr. Livermore's motion, and passed in the affirmative, thirty-one for, and twenty against it.

APPENDIX B[1]
TO THE HONORABLE THE GENERAL ASSEMBLY
OF THE COMMONWEALTH OF VIRGINIA
A MEMORIAL AND REMONSTRANCE AGAINST
RELIGIOUS ASSESSMENTS

We the subscribers, citizens of the said Commonwealth, having taken into serious consideration, a Bill printed by order of the last Session of General Assembly, entitled "A Bill establishing a provision for Teachers of the Christian Religion," and conceiving that the same if finally armed with the sanctions of a law, will be a dangerous abuse of power, are bound as faithful members of a free State to remonstrate against it, and to declare the reasons by which we are determined. We remonstrate against the said Bill,

1. Because we hold it for a fundamental and undeniable truth, "that religion or the duty which we owe to our Creator and the manner of discharging it, can be directed only by reason and conviction, not by force or violence." The Religion then of every man must be left to the conviction and conscience of every man; and it is the right of every man to exercise it as these may dictate. This right is in its nature an unalienable right. It is unalienable, because the opinions of men, depending only on the evidence contemplated by their own minds cannot follow the dictates of other men: It is unalienable also, because what is here a right towards men, is a duty towards the Creator. It is the duty of every man to render to the Creator such homage and such only as he believes to be acceptable to him. This duty is precedent, both in order of time and in degree of obligation, to the claims of Civil Society. Before any man can be considered as a member of Civil Society, he must be considered as a subject of the Governour of the Universe: And if a member of Civil Society, do it with a saving of his allegiance to the Universal Sovereign. We maintain therefore that in matters of Religion, no man's right is abridged by the institution of Civil Society and that Religion is wholly exempt from its cognizance. True it is, that no other rule exists, by which any question which may divide a Society, can be ultimately determined, but the will of the majority; but it is also true that the majority may trespass on the rights of the minority.

2. Because Religion be exempt from the authority of the Society at large, still less can it be subject to that of the Legislative Body. The latter are but the creatures and vicegerents of the former. Their jurisdiction is both derivative and limited: it is limited with regard to the co-ordinate departments, more necessarily is it limited with regard to the constituents. The preservation of a free Government requires not merely, that the metes and bounds which separate each department of power be invariably maintained; but more especially that neither of them be suffered to overleap the great Barrier which defends the rights of the people. The Rulers who are guilty of such an encroachment, exceed the commission from which they derive their authority, and are Tyrants. The People who submit to it are governed by laws made neither by themselves nor by an authority derived from them, and are slaves.

3. Because it is proper to take alarm at the first experiment on our liberties. We hold this prudent jealousy to be the first duty of Citizens, and one of the noblest characteristics of the late Revolution. The free men of America did not wait till usurped power had strengthened itself by exercise, and entangled the question in precedents. They saw all the consequences in the principle, and they avoided the consequences by denying the principle. We revere this lesson too much soon to forget it. Who does not see that the same authority which can establish Christianity, in exclusion of all other Religions, may establish with the same ease any particular sect of Christians, in exclusion of all other Sects? That the same authority which can force a citizen to contribute three pence only of his property for the support of any one establishment, may force him to conform to any other establishment in all cases whatsoever?

4. Because the Bill violates the equality which ought to be the basis of every law, and which is more indispensable, in proportion as the validity or expediency of any law is more liable to be impeached. If "all men are by nature equally free and independent," all men are to be considered as entering into Society on equal conditions; as relinquishing no more, and therefore retaining no less, one than another, of their natural rights. Above all are they to be considered as retaining an "equal title to the free exercise of Religion according to the dictates of Conscience." Whilst we assert for ourselves a freedom to embrace, to profess and to observe the Religion which we believe to be of divine origin, we cannot deny an equal freedom to those whose minds have not yet yielded to the evidence which has convinced us. If this freedom be abused, it is an offence against God, not against man: To God, therefore, not to man, must an account of it be rendered. As the Bill violates equality by subjecting some to peculiar burdens, so it violates the same principle, by granting to others peculiar exemptions. Are the Quakers and Menonists the only sects who think a compulsive support of their Religions unnecessary and unwarrantable? Can their piety alone be entrusted with the care of public worship? Ought their Religions to be endowed above all others with extraordinary privileges by which proselytes may be enticed from all others? We think too favorably of the justice and good sense of these denominations to believe that they either covet pre-eminences over their fellow citizens or that they will be seduced by them from the common opposition to the measure.

5. Because the Bill implies either that the Civil Magistrate is a competent Judge of Religious Truth; or that he may employ Religion as an engine of Civil policy. The first is an arrogant pretension falsified by the contradictory opinions of Rulers in all ages, and throughout the world: the second an unhallowed perversion of the means of salvation.

6. Because the establishment proposed by the Bill is not requisite for the support of the Christian Religion. To say that it is, is a contradiction to the Christian Religion itself, for every page of it disavows a dependence on the powers of this world: it is a contradiction to fact; for it is known that this Religion both existed and flourished, not only without the support of human laws, but in spite of every opposition from them, and not only during the period of miraculous aid, but long after it had been left to its own evidence and the ordinary care of Providence. Nay, it is a contradiction in terms; for a Religion not invented by human policy, must have pre-existed and been supported, before it was established by human policy. It is moreover to weaken in those who profess this Religion a pious confidence in its innate excellence and the patronage of its Author; and to foster in those who still reject it, a suspicion that its friends are too conscious of its fallacies to trust it to its own merits.

7. Because experience witnesseth that ecclesiastical establishments, instead of maintaining the purity and efficacy of Religion, have had a contrary operation. During almost fifteen centuries has the legal establishment of Christianity been on trial. What have been its fruits? More or less in all places, pride and indolence in the Clergy, ignorance and servility in the laity, in both, superstition, bigotry and persecution. Enquire of the Teachers of Christianity for the ages in which it appeared in its greatest lustre; those of every sect, point to the ages prior to its incorporation with Civil policy. Propose a restoration of this primitive State in which its Teachers depended on the voluntary rewards of their flocks, many of them predict its downfall. On which Side ought their testimony to have greatest weight, when for or when against their interest?

8. Because the establishment in question is not necessary for the support of Civil Government. If it be urged as necessary for the support of Civil Government only as it is a means of supporting Religion, and it be not necessary for the latter purpose, it cannot be necessary for the former. If Religion be not within the cognizance of Civil Government how can its legal establishment be necessary to Civil Government? What influence in fact have ecclesiastical establishments had on Civil Society?

In some instances they have been seen to erect a spiritual tyranny on the ruins of the Civil authority; in many instances they
have been seen upholding the thrones of political tyranny: in
no instance have they been seen the guardians of the liberties
of the people. Rulers who wished to subvert the public liberty,
may have found an established Clergy convenient auxiliaries.
A just Government instituted to secure & perpetuate it needs
them not. Such a Government will be best supported by protecting every Citizen in the enjoyment of his Religion with the
same equal hand which protects his person and his property;
by neither invading the equal rights of any Sect, nor suffering
any Sect to invade those of another.

9. Because the proposed establishment is a departure from the
generous policy, which, offering an Asylum to the persecuted
and oppressed of every Nation and Religion, promised a lustre
to our country, and an accession to the number of its citizens.
What a melancholy mark is the Bill of sudden degeneracy? Instead of holding forth an Asylum to the persecuted, it is itself a
signal of persecution. It degrades from the equal rank of Citizens all those whose opinions in Religion do not bend to those
of the Legislative authority. Distant as it may be in its present
form from the Inquisition, it differs from it only in degree. The
one is the first step, the other the last in the career of intoler-
ance. The magnanimous sufferer under this cruel scourge in
foreign Regions, must view the Bill as a Beacon on our Coast,
warning him to seek some other haven, where liberty and phi-
lanthropy in their due extent, may offer a more certain repose
from his Troubles.

10. Because it will have a like tendency to banish our Citizens.
The allurements presented by other situations are every day
thinning their number. To superadd a fresh motive to emigra-
tion by revoking the liberty which they now enjoy, would be the
same species of folly which has dishonoured and depopulated
flourishing kingdoms

11. Because it will destroy that moderation and harmony which the forbearance of our laws to intermeddle with Religion has produced among its several sects. Torrents of blood have been split in the old world, by vain attempts of the secular arm, to extinguish Religious discord, by proscribing all difference in Religious opinion. Time has at length revealed the true remedy. Every relaxation of narrow and rigorous policy, wherever it has been tried, has been found to assuage the disease. The American Theatre has exhibited proofs that equal and compleat liberty, if it does not wholly eradicate it, sufficiently destroys its malignant influence on the health and prosperity of the State. If with the salutary effects of this system under our own eyes, we begin to contract the bounds of Religious freedom, we know no name that will too severely reproach our folly. At least let warning be taken at the first fruits of the threatened innovation. The very appearance of the Bill has transformed "that Christian forbearance, love and charity," which of late mutually prevailed, into animosities and jeolousies, which may not soon be appeased. What mischiefs may not be dreaded, should this enemy to the public quiet be armed with the force of a law?

12. Because the policy of the Bill is adverse to the diffusion of the light of Christianity. The first wish of those who enjoy this precious gift ought to be that it may be imparted to the whole race of mankind. Compare the number of those who have as yet received it with the number still remaining under the dominion of false Religions; and how small is the former! Does the policy of the Bill tend to lessen the disproportion? No; it at once discourages those who are strangers to the light of revelation from coming into the Region of it; and countenances by example the nations who continue in darkness, in shutting out those who might convey it to them. Instead of Levelling as far as possible, every obstacle to the victorious progress of Truth, the Bill with an ignoble and unchristian timidity would circumscribe it with a wall of defence against the encroachments of error.

13. Because attempts to enforce by legal sanctions, acts obnoxious to so great a proportion of Citizens, tend to enervate the laws in general, and to slacken the bands of Society. If it be difficult to execute any law which is not generally deemed necessary or salutary, what must be the case, where it is deemed invalid and dangerous? And what may be the effect of so striking an example of impotency in the Government, on its general authority?

14. Because a measure of such singular magnitude and delicacy ought not to be imposed, without the clearest evidence that it is called for by a majority of citizens, and no satisfactory method is yet proposed by which the voice of the majority in this case may be determined, or its influence secured. The people of the respective counties are indeed requested to signify their opinion respecting the adoption of the Bill to the next Session of Assembly." But the representatives or of the Counties will be that of the people. Our hope is that neither of the former will, after due consideration, espouse the dangerous principle of the Bill. Should the event disappoint us, it will still leave us in full confidence, that a fair appeal to the latter will reverse the sentence against our liberties.

15. Because finally, "the equal right of every citizen to the free exercise of his Religion according to the dictates of conscience" is held by the same tenure with all our other rights. If we recur to its origin, it is equally the gift of nature; if we weigh its importance, it cannot be less dear to us; if we consult the "Declaration of those rights which pertain to the good people of Virginia, as the basis and foundation of Government," it is enumerated with equal solemnity, or rather studied emphasis. Either we must say, that the Will of the Legislature is the only measure of their authority; and that in the plenitude of this authority, they may sweep away all our fundamental rights; or, that they are bound to leave this particular right untouched and sacred: Either we must say, that they may controul the freedom of the press, may abolish the Trial by Jury, may swallow up the Executive and Judiciary Powers of the State; nay that they may despoil us of our very right of suffrage, and erect themselves into an independent and hereditary Assembly or, we must say, that they have no authority to enact into the law the Bill under consideration.

We the Subscribers say, that the General Assembly of this Commonwealth have no such authority: And that no effort may be omitted on our part against so dangerous an usurpation, we oppose to it, this remonstrance; earnestly praying, as we are in duty bound, that the Supreme Lawgiver of the Universe, by illuminating those to whom it is addressed, may on the one hand, turn their Councils from every act which would affront his holy prerogative, or violate the trust committed to them: and on the other, guide them into every measure which may be worthy of his [blessing, may re]dound to their own praise, and may establish more firmly the liberties, the prosperity and the happiness of the Commonwealth.

END NOTES

Chapter One

[1] See Chief Justice Renquist's opinion in *Van Orden v. Perry*, No 13-1500, slip op. at 9 (Sup. Ct., June 27, 2005) for a description of the places the Ten Commandments appear in the Supreme Court building.

[2] The population is taken from the Greater Madison Convention and Visitors Bureau website at http://www.visitmadison.com/visitorinfo/index.php?category_id=1&subcategory_id=3 (accessed January 13, 2006). The information about Madison religious groups is taken from the following sources: John-Brian Paprock, "Religious Diversity Graces Area," The Capital Times, Aug. 20, 1999: available at http://www.madison.com/archives/read.php?ref=tct:1999:08:20:205084:Lifestyle (accessed January 21, 2006); areaConnect, "Madison Wisconsin Churches and Religion Resources," http://madisonwi.areaconnect.com/churches.htm (accessed December 29, 2006).

Chapter Two

[1] These facts come from the Supreme Court opinion and from lower court opinions in the same case. See *Elk Grove Unified Sch. Dist. v. Newdow*, 542 U.S. 1 (2004); *Newdow v. United States Cong.*, 313 F.3d 500 (9th Cir. 2002); *Newdow v. United States Cong.*, 292 F.3d 597 (9th Cir. 2002).

[2] The courts' jurisdictional requirements, which determine where a case can be filed, are beyond the scope of this discussion.

[3] The U.S. Constitution provides for the Supreme Court but leaves it up to Congress to decide how the lower court system will function. From 1948 through 1976 most constitutional challenges were heard by panels of three district court judges and went straight from there to the Supreme Court. Congress changed the statute authorizing this procedure in 1976, so constitutional challenges now follow the normal route through the federal court system.

[4] This description reflects what usually happens, but each state adopts its own procedures, and there can be variations.

[5] For example, Vermont, Nevada, and South Dakota do not have an intermediate appeals court.

[6] The United States and its territories are geographically divided into twelve circuits—eleven numbered circuits and the District of Columbia.

[7] See *Elk Grove Unified Sch. Dist. v. Newdow*, 542 U.S. 1 (2004); *Rescue Army v. Mun. Court*, 331 U.S. 549 (1947); *Spector Motor Service v. McLaughlin*, 323 U.S. 101 (1944).

[8] *Ohio Civil Rights Comm'n v. Dayton Christian Sch., Inc.*, 477 U.S. 619 (1986).

[9] *Rescue Army*, n. 7. See also *Musser v. Utah*, 333 U.S. 95 (1948) (sending convictions for conspiracy to commit polygamy back to the Utah Supreme

Court so that it could interpret the meaning of a statute making it a crime to conspire to commit acts "injurious to ... public morals").

[10] *NLRB v. Catholic Bishop of Chicago,* 440 U.S. 490 (1979). See also *St. Martin Lutheran Church v. South Dakota,* 451 U.S. 772 (1981) (holding that the Federal Unemployment Tax Act exempted employees of church-operated schools from unemployment taxes, thereby avoiding the First Amendment issue).

[11] See *Lujan v. Defenders of Wildlife,* 504 U.S. 555 (1992); *Allen v. Wright,* 468 U.S. 737 (1984); *Flast v. Cohen,* 392 U.S. 83 (1968). Although these are federal cases, states generally use similar tests.

[12] *Doremus v. Bd. of Educ.,* 342 U.S. 429 (1952).

[13] *Newdow,* n. 7.

[14] *Engel v. Vitale,* 370 U.S. 421 (1962).

[15] See *Agostini v. Felton,* 521 U.S. 203 (1997); *Helvering v. Hallock,* 309 U.S. 106 (1940).

[16] See *Burnet v. Coronado Oil & Gas Co.,* 285 U.S. 393, 406 (1932) (Brandeis, J., dissenting), overruled by *Helvering v. Mountain Producers Corp.,* 303 U.S. 376 (1938).

[17] *Agostini,* n. 15; *Planned Parenthood v. Casey,* 505 U.S. 833 (1992); *Helvering v. Hallock,* n. 15.

[18] *West Virginia Bd. of Educ. v. Barnette,* 319 U.S. 624 (1943).

[19] See *Minersville Sch. Dist. v. Gobitis,* 310 U.S. 586 (1940).

[20] *Barnette,* n. 18, at 643 (Black, J., concurring) (internal citation omitted).

[21] *Mitchell v. Helms,* 530 U.S. 793 (2000); *Agostini,* n. 15.

[22] See *Lamie v. United States Trustee,* 540 U.S. 526 (2004); *Hughes Aircraft Co. v. Jacobson,* 525 U.S. 432 (1999); *Robinson v. Shell Oil Co.,* 519 U.S. 337 (1997); *United States v. Ron Pair Enterprises, Inc.,* 489 U.S. 235 (1989); *Am. Tobacco Co. v. Patterson,* 456 U.S. 63 (1982); *United States. v. Pub. Utilities Comm'n,* 345 U.S. 295 (1953).

[23] *Perrin v. United States,* 444 U.S. 37 (1979). See also *Amoco Production Co. v. S. Ute Indian Tribe,* 526 U.S. 865 (1999); *FDIC v. Meyer,* 510 U.S. 471 (1994); *Am. Tobacco Co.,* n. 22.

[24] *Marbury v. Madison,* 5 U.S. 137 (1803); but see *Lamie,* n. 22 (holding that a word may be surplusage if it is inadvertently included, makes the provision conflict with the rest of the law, or is inconsistent with the otherwise plain meaning of the provision).

[25] *Lamie,* n. 22.

[26] *Trustees of Dartmouth Coll. v. Woodward,* 17 U.S. 518 (1819).

[27] Ibid., 644-645.

[28] *Blum v. Stenson,* 465 U.S. 886 (1984); *Pub. Utilities Comm'n,* n. 22;.

Chapter Three

[1] Article VI, Clause 3 prohibited the new government from requiring a religious test as a condition for holding office. There were no other provisions that mentioned religion.

[2] Proceedings of the Constitutional Convention on September 12, 1787, in Bernard Schwartz, comp., *The Bill of Rights: A Documentary History*, Vol. I (New York: Chelsea House Publishers, 1971), 438.

[3] Schwartz, *The Bill of Rights*, Vol. I, 438. The quotations regarding comments made by the delegates are from the Convention record, but those records only paraphrase the debates.

[4] Ibid., 439.

[5] Madison to Jefferson, New York, October 24, 1787, in *The Republic of Letters: The Correspondence between Thomas Jefferson and James Madison 1776–1826*, Vol. 1, ed. James Morton Smith, (New York: W.W. Norton & Company, 1995), 503.

[6] Jefferson to Francis Hopkinson, Paris, March 13, 1789, in Schwartz, *The Bill of Rights*, Vol. I, 618-619.

[7] Jefferson to Madison, Paris, December 20, 1787, *The Republic of Letters*, Vol. I, 512–513.

[8] Ibid, 513.

[9] Jefferson to Willlliam Stephens Smith, Paris, February 1788, in Schwartz, *The Bill of Rights*, Vol. I, 609; Jefferson to Madison, Paris, February 6, 1788, in *The Republic of Letters*, 529–530; Jefferson to Alexander Donald, Paris, February 7, 1788, in Schwartz, *The Bill of Rights*, Vol. I, 611–612; Jefferson to C.W.F. Dumas, Paris, February 12, 1788, in Schwartz, *The Bill of Rights*, Vol. I, 613.

[10] See Madison to Jefferson, New York, October 17, 1788, in *The Republic of Letters*, Vol. I, 564 (emphasis in the original letter). See also Madison's speech to Congress proposing the bill of rights, *Annals of Congress* in Schwartz, *The Bill of Rights*, Vol. II, 1028 ("I will own that I never considered this provision so essential to the federal constitution, as to make it improper to ratify it, until such an amendment was added; at the same time, I always conceived, that in a certain form, and to a certain extent, such a provision was neither improper nor altogether useless.").

[11] Jefferson to Madison, Paris, March 15, 1789, in *The Republic of Letters*, Vol. I, 587. Jefferson trusted the Court so much that if he had had his way, the Constitution would have given the Court a veto over legislation passed by Congress. "I like the negative given to the Executive with a third of either house, though I should have liked it better had the Judiciary been associated for that purpose, or invested with a similar and separate power." December 20, 1787 letter from Jefferson to Madison, Paris, December 20, 1787, in Schwartz, *The Republic of Letters*, Vol. I, 512.

[12] Schwartz, *The Bill of Rights*, Vol. II, 664.

[13] Ibid., 735.

[14] Ibid., 761.

[15] Ibid., 842.

[16] Ibid., 912.

[17] Ibid., 968.

[18] *Annals of Congress*, in Schwartz, *The Bill of Rights*, Vol. II, 1031. The *Annals* is available on the Library of Congress web site at http://memory.loc.gov/ammem/amlaw/lawhome.html.

[19] Ibid., 1026.

[20] Ibid., 1088.

[21] Ibid., 1064.

[22] Ibid., 1088.

[23] *House of Representatives Journal*, in Schwartz, *The Bill of Rights*, Vol. II, 1122; *Senate Journal*, in Schwartz, *The Bill of Rights*, Vol. II, 1148. Both *Journals* are available on the Library of Congress web site at http://memory.loc.gov/ammem/amlaw/lawhome.html.

[24] Ibid., 1153.

[25] *House of Representatives Journal*, in Schwartz, *The Bill of Rights*, Vol, II, 1160; *Senate Journal*, in Schwartz, *The Bill of Rights*, Vol. II, 1164.

[26] Actually, Virginia appears to have ratified the first of the twelve amendments on November 3, 1791.

[27] The second amendment was eventually ratified. It became the 27th Amendment in 1992.

[28] *Everson v. Bd. of Educ.*, 330 U.S. 1, 26 (1947) (Jackson, J., dissenting).

Chapter Four

[1] "James Madison's Autobiography," edited by Douglass Adair, *William and Mary Quarterly*, 3rd Series, Vol. 2 (1945), 199 (emphasis in original document).

[2] For a brief history of religion in early America, see the Library of Congress online exhibit "Religion and the Founding of the American Republic," located at http://www.loc.gov/exhibits/religion/. According to the Library of Congress online exhibit "From Haven to Home: 350 Years of Jewish Life in America," there were between 1,000 and 2,500 Jews in America in 1776. See the timeline at http://www.loc.gov/exhibits/haventohome/timeline/haven-timeline_1.html.

[3] Bernard Schwartz, comp., *The Bill of Rights: A Documentary History*, Vol. I, (New York: Chelsea House Publishers, 1971), 229.

[4] Ibid., 236.

[5] Ibid., 299.

[6] Ibid., 312.

[7] Ibid., 287.

[8] Ibid., 277.

[9] Ibid., 267.

[10] Ibid., 283–284.

[11] Ibid., 260.

[12] Ibid., 340.

[13] Ibid., 340-341, 375–376.

[14] Ibid., 322.

[15] Ibid., 326–331.

[16] Ibid., 333–334.

[17] Ibid., 289.

[18] See letter from Madison to Jefferson, Richmond, January 9, 1785, in *The Republic of Letters*, Vol. I, 361; "Madison's 'Detached Memoranda,'" edited by Elizabeth Fleet, *William and Mary Quarterly*, 3rd Series, Vol. 3 (1946), 561.

[19] James Madison, "Memorial and Remonstrance Against Religious Assessments," 1785, available on the University of Virginia Library web site at http://religiousfreedom.lib.virginia.edu/sacred/madison_m&r_1785. html (accessed January 20, 2006). An image of the original handwritten document can be viewed on the Library of Congress web site at http://memory.loc.gov/master/mss/mjm/02/0400/0449d.jpg.

[20] "The Virginia Act for Establishing Religious Freedom," available on the University of Virginia Library web site at http://religiousfreedom.lib. virginia.edu/sacred/vaact.html (accessed January 20, 2006).

[21] "Madison's 'Detached Memoranda,'" n. 18, 556. The Memoranda is not dated and could have been written any time between the end of Madison's presidency in 1817 and his death in 1836.

[22] Danbury Baptist Association to Jefferson, Connecticut, October 7, 1801. An image of the letter can be viewed on the Library of Congress web site at http://memory.loc.gov/master/mss/mtj/mtj1/024/0900/0956.jpg.

[23] Jefferson to Danbury Baptist Association, January 1, 1802. An image of the final letter can be viewed on the Library of Congress web site at http://memory.loc.gov/master/mss/mtj/mtj1/025/0500/0558.jpg. An image of the draft letter can be viewed on the Library of Congress web site at http://memory.loc.gov/master/mss/mtj/mtj1/025/0500/0557.jpg.

[24] See *McCollum v. Bd. of Educ.*, 333 U.S. 203, 211 (1948); *Everson v. Bd. of Educ.*, 330 U.S. 1, 15–16 (1947); *Reynolds v. United States*, 98 U.S. 145, 164 (1878).

[25] Jefferson to Danbury Baptist Association, n. 23.

[26] James Hutson, "'A Wall of Separation,' FBI Helps Restore Jefferson's Obliterated Draft," Library of Congress Information Bulletin, June 1998, available at www.loc.gov/loc/lcib/9806/danbury.html (accessed January 20, 2006).

[27] "Madison's 'Detached Memoranda,'" n. 18, 555.

[28] *Annals of Congress*, 1st Congress, 1st Session, 241, available on the Library of Congress web site at http://memory.loc.gov/ammem/amlaw/lawhome. html.

[29] *Annals of Congress*, 1st Congress, 3rd Session, 2415.

[30] "Madison's 'Detached Memoranda,'" n. 18, 558.

[31] Ibid., 559.

[32] "James Madison's Autobiography," n. 1, 204.

[33] "Memorial and Remonstrance," n. 19.

Chapter Five

[1] See, for example, *Reynolds v. United States*, 89 U.S. 145 (1878); *Davis v. Beason*, 133 U.S. 333 (1890), abrogated in part by *Romer v. Evans*, 517 U.S. 620

(1996); *Late Corp. of the Church of Jesus Christ of the Latter-Day Saints v. United States*, 136 U.S. 1 (1890). These cases are discussed in Chapter Eight.

[2] *Reuben Quick Bear v. Leupp*, 210 U.S. 50 (1908). This case is discussed in Chapter Eight.

[3] These cases began with *Lovell v. Griffin*, 303 U.S. 444 (1938), a case involving religious speech that is discussed in Chapter Ten.

[4] *Terrett v. Taylor*, 13 U.S. 43 (1815).

[5] Ibid., 49.

[6] *Mason v. Muncaster*, 22 U.S. 445 (1824).

[7] *Ponce v. Roman Catholic Apostolic Church*, 210 U.S. 296 (1908).

[8] *Missionary Society of M.E. Church v. Dalles City*, 107 U.S. 336 (1883).

[9] *Corp. of the Catholic Bishop of Nesqually v. Gibbon*, 158 U.S. 155 (1895).

[10] *Goesele v. Bimeler*, 55 U.S. 589 (1952).

[11] *Baker v. Nachtrieb*, 60 U.S. 126 (1856).

[12] *Order of St. Benedict v. Steinhauser*, 234 U.S. 640 (1914).

[13] Father Wirth probably did not have a will since his estate was handled by an administrator. Estates left by will are usually handled by executors.

[14] *Vidal v. Philadelphia*, 43 U.S. 127 (1844).

[15] Ibid., 133.

[16] Ibid., 198.

[17] Ibid., 201.

[18] *Lowrey v. Territory of Hawaii*, 206 U.S. 206 (1907); *Lowrey v. Territory of Hawaii*, 215 U.S. 554 (1910).

[19] *Lowrey I*, n. 18, 224.

[20] *Meyer v. Nebraska*, 262 U.S. 390 (1923). See also *Bartels v. Iowa*, 262 U.S. 404 (1923).

[21] *Meyer*, n. 20, 401.

[22] Ibid., 403.

[23] *Pierce v. Society of the Sisters of the Holy Names of Jesus and Mary*, 268 U.S. 510 (1925).

[24] Ibid., 534-535.

[25] *Cochran v. Louisiana State Bd. of Educ.*, 281 U.S. 370 (1930).

[26] Ibid., 375.

[27] *Permoli v. New Orleans*, 44 U.S. 589 (1845).

[28] The decision does not say why the ordinance was adopted, but there are some indications that it may have been a way for the people in charge of the obituary chapel to charge fees they would not receive if the funeral were held in a church.

[29] *Permoli*, n. 27, 609.

[30] *Hallett v. Collins*, 51 U.S. 174 (1850).

[31] *Cummings v. Missouri*, 71 U.S. 277 (1866).

[32] The oath did not actually identify the sides as the Confederacy and the Union but merely referred to taking up arms against or avoiding service for the United States. It is not clear from the case just what part of the oath Rev. Cummings felt he could not take.

[33] U.S. Constitution, art. I, sec. 10, cl. 1.

[34] *Cummings,* n. 31, 313-314. As was the custom at the time, the Court's official reporter summarized the parties' arguments before printing the Court's opinion.

[35] *Church of the Holy Trinity v. United States,* 143 U.S. 457 (1892).

[36] Ibid., 465.

[37] Ibid., 471.

[38] *Bradfield v. Roberts,* 175 U.S. 291 (1899).

[39] See also *Speer v. Colbert,* 200 U.S. 130 (1906) (finding that a college and two orphan asylums run by religious orders were not religious institutions).

[40] *Hygrade Provision Co. v. Sherman,* 266 U.S. 497 (1925).

Chapter Six

[1] These facts come from the Supreme Court opinions (including concurring and dissenting opinions) and from lower court decisions in the same case. See *Sch. Dist. v. Schempp,* 374 U.S. 203 (1963); *Schempp v. Sch. Dist.,* 201 F.Supp. 815 (E.D.Pa. 1962); *Schempp v. Sch. Dist.,* 177 F.Supp. 398 (1959).

[2] *Everson v. Bd. of Educ.,* 330 U.S. 1 (1947) (cite omitted, italics in original).

[3] Ibid., 18.

[4] Ibid., 15–16.

[5] Ibid., 31–32.

[6] *Lemon v. Kurtzman,* 403 U.S. 602 (1971).

[7] *Agostini v. Felton,* 521 U.S. 203 (1997).

[8] *Engel v. Vitale,* 370 U.S. 421 (1962).

[9] Ibid., 423.

[10] Ibid., 430–431.

[11] See *Sch. Dist. v. Schempp,* 374 U.S. 203 (1963). The Court decided the companion case of *Murray v. Curlett* with *Schempp* at the Supreme Court level.

[12] Ibid., 222.

[13] *Wallace v. Jaffree,* 472 U.S. 38 (1985).

[14] *Lee v. Weisman,* 505 U.S. 577 (1992).

[15] *Santa Fe Indep. Sch. Dist. v. Doe,* 530 U.S. 290 (2000).

[16] The prayer decisions also recognize that subtle coercion has a greater effect on children than on adults. Based on this principle, the Court has allowed prayer in state legislatures but not in public elementary and secondary schools. Compare *Marsh v. Chambers,* 463 U.S. 783 (1983) with *Doe,* n. 15; *Lee,* n. 14; *Wallace,* n. 13; *Schempp,* n. 11; *Engel,* n. 8.

[17] Ibid., 42 (internal cite omitted).

[18] *Stone v. Graham,* 449 U.S. 39 (1980).

[19] Ibid., 313.

[20] *Epperson v. Arkansas,* 393 U.S. 97 (1968). From the Court's discussion of the facts, it seems that the Arkansas statute had been on the books for years and had never been enforced. And, apparently, state officials still had no

desire to enforce it. The case appears to have been designed to test the law, and Susan Epperson appears to have been a willing volunteer.

[21] Ibid., 106.

[22] Ibid., 107.

[23] *Edwards v. Aguillard,* 482 U.S. 578 (1987).

[24] Ibid., 593.

[25] *McCollum v. Bd. of Educ.,* 333 U.S. 203 (1948).

[26] *Zorach v. Clauson,* 343 U.S. 306 (1952).

[27] The Supreme Court has also made it clear that school authorities do not violate the Establishment Clause when they allow religious groups to use school facilities for after-school activities on the same terms as other groups. In fact, as discussed in later chapters, a school may violate other provisions of the First Amendment if it gives secular groups access to its facilities but denies access to religious groups. See *Good News Club v. Milford Cent. Sch.,* 533 U.S. 98 (2001); *Rosenberger v. Rector of Univ. of Virginia,* 515 U.S. 819 (1995); *Lamb's Chapel v. Ctr. Moriches Union Free Sch. Dist.,* 508 U.S. 384 (1993); *Bd. of Educ. v. Mergens,* 496 U.S. 226 (1990); *Widmar v. Vincent,* 454 U.S. 263 (1981).

[28] *Everson,* n. 2.

[29] *Bd. of Educ. v. Allen,* 392 U.S. 236 (1968).

[30] *Lemon,* n. 6.

[31] Ibid., 618.

[32] *Witters v. Washington Dept. of Services for the Blind,* 474 U.S. 481 (1986).

[33] *Witters v. Washington Comm'n for the Blind,* 112 Wash.2d 363, 771 P.2d 1119 (1989). The Washington Supreme Court also held that denying the assistance did not violate the Free Exercise Clause, and this time the U.S. Supreme Court refused to hear it. See *Witters v. Washington Dept. of Services for the Blind,* 493 U.S. 850 (1989) (denying cert.). As will be discussed in Chapter Eight, the U.S. Supreme Court addressed the Free Exercise question fifteen years later in *Locke v. Davey,* 540 U.S. 712 (2004).

[34] *Zobrest v. Catalina Foothills Sch. Dist.,* 509 U.S. 1 (1993).

[35] *Agostini,* n. 7.

[36] *Mitchell v. Helms,* 530 U.S. 793 (2000).

[37] *Agostini,* n. 7, overruling *Aguilar v. Felton,* 473 U.S. 402 (1985) and parts of *Sch. Dist. v. Ball,* 473 U.S. 373 (1985); *Mitchell,* n. 35, overruling *Meek v. Pittenger,* 421 U.S. 349 (1975) and *Wolman v. Walter,* 433 U.S. 229 (1977).

[38] *Lemon,* n. 6.

[39] *Levitt v. Comm. for Pub. Educ. and Religious Liberty,* 413 U.S. 472 (1973).

[40] *Comm. for Pub. Educ. and Religious Liberty v. Nyquist,* 413 U.S. 756 (1973).

[41] Ibid.; *Sloan v. Lemon,* 413 U.S. 825 (1973).

[42] *Nyquist,* n. 39.

[43] *Everson,* n. 2.

[44] *Allen,* n. 29.

[45] *Comm. for Pub. Educ. and Religious Liberty v. Regan,* 444 U.S. 646 (1980).

[46] Ibid.

[47] *Mueller v. Allen*, 463 U.S. 388 (1983).

[48] *Zobrest*, n. 33.

[49] *Agostini*, n. 7.

[50] *Mitchell*, n. 35.

[51] *Zelman v. Simmons-Harris*, 536 U.S. 639 (2002).

[52] *Roemer v. Bd. of Pub. Works*, 426 U.S. 736 (1976); *Hunt v. McNair*, 413 U.S. 734 (1973); *Tilton v. Richardson*, 403 U.S. 672 (1971).

[53] *Tilton*, n. 51, 685–686 (internal citation and footnotes omitted).

[54] *Bd. of Educ. v. Grumet*, 512 U.S. 687 (1994).

[55] Ibid., 703 (footnote omitted).

Chapter Seven

[1] These facts come from the Supreme Court opinions (including concurring and dissenting opinions), lower court decisions in the same case, contemporaneous news articles, and the records of the State Bar of Texas. See *Van Orden v. Perry*, No 13–1500 (Sup. Ct., June 27, 2005); *Van Orden v. Perry*, 351 F.3d 173 (5th Cir. 2003); *Van Orden v. Perry*, 2002 WL 32737462 (W.D.Tex. 2002); Sylvia Morano, "Supreme Court on a Shoestring," *Washington Post*, February 21, 2005; Polly Ross Hughes, "Church-State Dispute Hits Home," *Houston Chronicle*, September 14, 2003; Texas State Bar Records for Thomas D. Van Orden, http://www.texasbar.com (accessed July 26, 2005).

[2] *Stone v. Graham*, 449 U.S. 39 (1980).

[3] *Lynch v. Donnelly*, 465 U.S. 668 (1984).

[4] *County of Allegheny v. ACLU*, 492 U.S. 573 (1989).

[5] *McCreary County v. ACLU*, No 03–1693, (Sup. Ct. Jun. 27, 2005).

[6] *Van Orden v. Perry*, No. 03–1500 (Sup. Ct. Jun. 27, 2005).

[7] Ibid., slip opinion at 4 (plurality opinion).

[8] *Walz v. Tax Comm'n*, 397 U.S. 664 (1970).

[9] Ibid., 668–669.

[10] Ibid., 669.

[11] In *Gibbons v. District of Columbia*, 116 U.S. 404 (1886), the Court held that the District was not required to provide a tax exemption for income property owned by a church. The opinion does not mention the Establishment Clause.

[12] *Estate of Thornton v. Caldor, Inc.*, 472 U.S. 703 (1985). Thornton had died by the time the case reached the Supreme Court.

[13] *Corp. of Presiding Bishop v. Amos*, 483 U.S. 327 (1987).

[14] *Texas Monthly v. Bullock*, 489 U.S. 1 (1989).

[15] The next year the Court decided that imposing sales and use taxes on retail merchandise does not violate either the Establishment Clause or the Free Exercise Clause. *Swaggart Ministries v. California Bd. of Equalization*, 493 U.S. 378 (1990).

[16] *McGowan v. Maryland*, 366 U.S. 420 (1961). This discussion also includes three similar cases decided on the same day: *Two Guys From Harrison-Allen-*

town, Inc. v. McGinley, 366 U.S. 582 (1961); *Braunfeld v. Brown,* 366 U.S. 599 (1961); and *Gallagher v. Crown Kosher Market, Inc.,* 366 U.S. 617 (1961).

[17] *McGowan,* n. 14, 445.

[18] *Hennington v. Georgia,* 163 U.S. 299, 307 (1896). See also *Petit v. Minnesota,* 177 U.S. 164 (1900); *Bucher v. Cheshire R.R. Co.,* 125 U.S. 555 (1888); *Philadelphia, Wilmington, and Baltimore R.R. Co. v. The Philadelphia and Havre de Grace Steam Towboat Co.,* 64 U.S. 209 (1859); *Richardson v. Goodard,* 64 U.S. 28 (1859).

[19] *Torcaso v. Watkins,* 367 U.S. 488 (1961).

[20] Ibid., 495.

[21] *Larson v. Valente,* 456 U.S. 228 (1982).

[22] Ibid., 244.

[23] *Larkin v. Grendel's Den, Inc.,* 459 U.S. 116 (1982).

[24] Ibid., 127.

[25] Some of the many examples include *Sherbert v. Verner,* 374 U.S. 398 (1963) (state would not violate Establishment Clause by granting unemployment compensation benefits to Seventh Day Adventist who refused to accept Saturday work); *Widmar v. Vincent,* 454 U.S. 263 (1981) (university would not violate Establishment Clause by granting religious student groups access to university premises on the same basis as secular student groups); *Lamb's Chapel v. Ctr. Moriches Sch. Dist.,* 508 U.S. 384 (1993) (public school would not violate Establishment Clause by granting religious groups from the community access to school premises on the same basis as other community groups); *Zobrest v. Catalina Foothills Sch. Dist.,* 509 U.S. 1 (1993) (state would not violate Establishment Clause by providing a sign language interpreter to Catholic high school student on same basis as public school students); *Capitol Sq. Review Bd. v. Pinette,* 515 U.S. 753 (1995) (state would not violate Establishment Clause by allowing a group to set up a display involving a religious symbol in a public forum where other groups were allowed to set up secular displays); *Rosenberger v. Rector of Univ. of Virginia,* 515 U.S. 819 (1995) (university would not violate Establishment Clause by funding religious student publications on the same basis as other student publications).

Chapter Eight

[1] These facts are taken from the Supreme Court opinions (including Justice Stone's dissent) and from lower court decisions in the same case. See *Minersville Sch. Dist. v. Gobitis,* 310 U.S. 586 (1940); *Minersville Sch. Dist. v. Gobitis,* 108 F.2d 683 (3rd Cir. 1939); *Gobitis v. Minersville Sch. Dist.,* 24 F.Supp. 271 (E.D.Penn. 1938). See also Peter Irons, *The Courage of Their Convictions: Sixteen Americans Who Fought Their Way to the Supreme Court,* Penguin Books 1990, 15–35 (including recollections from Lillian Gobitis).

[2] See *Cantwell v. Connecticut,* 310 U.S. 296 (1940).

[3] *Gobitis,* n. 1.

[4] Ibid., 594, 595.

[5] Ibid., 605 (Stone, J., dissenting).

[6] *West Virginia Bd. of Ed. v. Barnette,* 319 U.S. 624 (1943).

[7] Justice Murphy was appointed to the Supreme Court two months before *Gobitis* was argued.

[8] See "Maine Crowd Beats Two Who Flout Flag," *New York Times,* June 9, 1940; "Prepared to Call Troups in Maine," *New York Times,* June 11, 1940; "Beaten on Refusal to Salute the Flag," *New York Times,* June 17, 1940. *Gobitis* was decided on June 3, 1940.

[9] *Barnette,* n. 8, 633–634.

[10] Ibid., 645 (Murphy, J., concurring).

[11] *Follett v. Town of McCormick,* 321 U.S. 573 (1944); *Jamison v. Texas,* 318 U.S. 413 (1943); *Chaplinsky v. New Hampshire,* 315 U.S. 568 (1942); *Cantwell,* n. 2; *Schneider v. New Jersey,* 308 U.S. 147 (1939); *Lovell v. City of Griffin,* 303 U.S. 444 (1938).

[12] *Cantwell,* n. 2.

[13] Ibid., 303-304.

[14] *Prince v. Massachusetts,* 321 U.S. 158 (1944).

[15] Ibid., 171.

[16] *Fowler v. Rhode Island,* 345 U.S. 67 (1953); *Niemotko v. Maryland,* 340 U.S. 268 (1951); *Cox v. New Hampshire,* 312 U.S. 569 (1941).

[17] *Niemotko,* n. 16.

[18] *Reynolds v. U.S.,* 89 U.S. 145 (1878).

[19] Ibid., 166–167.

[20] *Davis v. Beason,* 133 U.S. 333 (1890), abrogated in part by *Romer v. Evans,* 517 U.S. 620, 634 (1996) ("to the extent *Davis* held that persons advocating a certain practice may be denied the right to vote, it is no longer good law.")

[21] Although the Mormons consistently lost their First Amendment claims, they had more success with other, mostly procedural, arguments. See *Ex parte Nielsen,* 131 U.S. 176 (1889) (finding that Utah could not obtain two separate convictions for similar offences—adultery and unlawful cohabitation—that relied on the same evidence); *Ex parte Snow,* 120 U.S. 274 (1887) (finding that Utah violated Snow's rights when it divided a three-year polygamous relationship into three separate charges of a year each so that it could triple the sentence authorized by law); *Miles v. United States,* 103 U.S. 304 (1880) (throwing out inadmissible evidence of the polygamous relationship).

[22] *Late Corp. of the Church of Jesus Christ of Latter-Day Saints v. United States,* 136 U.S. 1 (1890).

[23] Ibid., 49-50.

[24] *Cleveland v. United States,* 329 U.S. 14 (1946).

[25] *Reuben Quick Bear v. Leupp,* 210 U.S. 50 (1908).

[26] *Torcaso v. Watkins,* 367 U.S. 488 (1961).

[27] *Cruz v. Beto,* 405 U.S. 319 (1972).

[28] Ibid., 322.

[29] *McDaniel v. Paty*, 435 U.S. 618 (1978).

[30] The other justice found that the Tennessee law violated the Equal Protection Clause of the Fourteenth Amendment.

[31] *Church of Lukumi Babalu Aye, Inc. v. City of Hialeah*, 508 U.S. 520 (1993).

[32] Ibid., 546.

[33] Ibid., 547.

[34] *Locke v. Davey*, 540 U.S. 712 (2004).

[35] See "Faith in the Law; The Supreme Court upholds religious discrimination" by Joshua Davey, *Education Next*, Summer 2004.

[36] *Braunfeld v. Brown*, 366 U.S. 599 (1961); *Gallagher v. Crown Kosher Market*, 366 U.S. 617 (1961).

[37] *Hernandez v. Comm'r of Internal Revenue*, 490 U.S. 680 (1989).

[38] See also *Swaggart Ministries v. Caifornia Bd. of Equalization*, 493 U.S. 378 (1990) (holding that the free exercise clause does not prevent a state from collecting sales taxes on religious items).

[39] *Tony & Susan Alamo Foundation v. Sec'y of Labor*, 471 U.S. 290 (1985).

[40] *Hamilton v. Regents of the Univ. of California*, 293 U.S. 245 (1934).

[41] *Thomas v. Review Bd. of Indiana Employment Sec. Div.*, 450 U.S. 707 (1981).

[42] Ibid., 714.

[43] *Frazee v. Illinois Employment Security Dept.*, 489 U.S. 829 (1989).

[44] *United States v. Ballard*, 322 U.S. 78 (1944).

[45] Ibid., 86–87.

[46] *Sherbert v. Verner*, 374 U.S. 398 (1963). See also *Frazee*, n. 43; *Hobbie v. Unemployment Appeals Comm'n*, 480 U.S. 136 (1987); *Thomas*, n. 41.

[47] *Sherbert*, n. 46.

[48] Ibid., 406.

[49] *Hobbie*, n. 46.

[50] *Wisconsin v. Yoder*, 406 U.S. 205 (1972).

[51] *United States v. Lee*. 455 U.S. 252 (1982).

[52] *Bob Jones Univ. v. United States*, 461 U.S. 574 (1983).

[53] Ibid., 604.

[54] *Bowen v. Roy*, 476 U.S. 693 (1986).

[55] Ibid., 699–700 (emphasis and brackets in original, citation omitted).

[56] *Lyng v. Nw. Indian Cemetery Ass'n*, 485 U.S. 439 (1988).

[57] *Employment Div. v. Smith*, 494 U.S. 872 (1990). The case had come to the U.S. Supreme Court once before and was sent back to the Oregon Supreme Court to decide whether the religious use of peyote was exempt from Oregon's criminal statute. *Employment Div. v. Smith*, 485 U.S. 660 (1988). The Oregon court decided it was not. *Smith v. Employment Div.*, 307 Or. 68, 763 P.2d 146 (1988).

[58] *Hobbie*, n. 46; *Thomas*, n. 41; *Sherbert*, n. 46.

[59] *Employment Div. v. Smith*, 494 U.S. 872, 878-879 (1990).

[60] Ibid., 883.

[61] Ibid., 891.

Chapter Nine

[1] *Employment Div. v. Smith*, 494 U.S. 872 (1990).

[2] This discussion is based on RFRA's legislative history. See H.R. Rep. No. 103–88 (1993); S. Rep. No. 103–111 (1993); 139 CONG. REC. S2823-24, S14350-68, S14470–71 (daily ed. Mar. 11, 1993, Oct. 26, 1993, Oct. 27, 1993); 139 CONG. REC. H2356–63, H8713–15 (daily ed. May 11, 1993, Nov. 3, 1993).

[3] *O'Lone v. Estate of Shabazz*, 482 U.S. 342 (1987).

[4] Ibid., 349.

[5] *Goldman v. Weinberger*, 475 U.S. 503 (1986).

[6] Congress had already rectified *Goldman* with legislation that addressed the military's right to affect religious conduct. See 10 U.S.C. Sec. 774.

[7] *City of Boerne v. Flores*, 521 U.S. 507 (1997).

[8] *Marbury v. Madison*, 5 U.S. 137 (1803).

[9] *Gonzales v. O Centro Espirita Beneficente Uniao Do Vegetal*, No. 04-1084 (Sup. Ct., Feb. 21, 2006).

[10] This discussion is based on RLUIPA's legislative history. See H.R. Rep. No. 106–219 (2000); 146 CONG. REC. S6687–90, S7774-81 (daily ed. Jul. 13, 2000, Jul. 27, 2000); 146 CONG. REC. E1234–35 (daily ed. Jul. 14, 2000); 146 CONG. REC. H7190–92 (daily ed. Jul. 27, 2000).

[11] *Cutter v. Wilkinson*, No. 03–9877 (Sup. Ct. Mar. 21, 2005).

Chapter Ten

[1] *Joseph Burstyn, Inc. v. Wilson*, 343 U.S. 495 (1952). The movie plot and other facts are taken from Justice Frankfurter's separate opinion concurring in the judgment.

[2] Ibid., 505.

[3] *Lovell v. City of Griffin*, 303 U.S. 444 (1938).

[4] Ibid., 451.

[5] *Schneider v. New Jersey*, 308 U.S. 147 (1939). See also *Largent v. Texas*, 318 U.S. 418 (1943).

[6] *Watchtower Bible & Tract Soc'y v. Village of Stratton*, 536 U.S. 150 (2002).

[7] Ibid, 165-166.

[8] *Saia v. New York*, 334 U.S. 558 (1948); *Follett v. Town of McCormick*, 321 U.S. 573 (1944); *Martin v. Struthers*, 319 U.S. 141 (1943); *Jones v. City of Opelika*, 319 U.S. 105 (1943); *Jamison v. Texas*, 318 U.S. 413 (1943). See also *Marsh v. Alabama*, 326 U.S. 501 (1946); *Busey v. District of Columbia*, 319 U.S. 579 (1943).

[9] *Cantwell v. Connecticut*, 310 U.S. 296 (1940).

[10] Ibid., 310.

[11] *Chaplinsky v. New Hampshire*, 315 U.S. 568 (1942).

[12] Ibid., 571–572 (quoting from *Cantwell*, n. 9).

[13] *Marsh*, n. 8. See also *Tucker v. Texas*, 326 U.S. 517 (1946).

[14] *Wooley v. Maynard*, 430 U.S. 705 (1977).

[15] Ibid., 714.

[16] Ibid., 715.

[17] *Cox v. New Hampshire*, 312 U.S. 569 (1941).

[18] Ibid., 576.

[19] *Niemotko v. Maryland*, 340 U.S. 268 (1951).

[20] *Fowler v. Rhode Island*, 345 U.S. 67 (1953).

[21] *Jamison*, n. 8, 416. See also *Kunz v. New York*, 340 U.S. 290 (1951) (holding that New York City could not arbitrarily deny a Baptist minister a license to preach on the city streets); *Cantwell*, n.9, 308 ("Jesse Cantwell . . . was upon a public street, where he had a right to be, and where he had a right peacefully to impart his views to others."); *Schneider*, n. 5, 160 (holding that legislation may not "abridge the constitutional liberty of one rightfully upon the street to impart information through speech or the distribution of literature").

[22] *Heffron v. Int'l Soc'y for Krishna Consciousness*, 452 U.S. 640 (1981).

[23] *Airport Comm'rs v. Jews for Jesus, Inc.*, 482 U.S. 569 (1987).

[24] *Int'l Soc'y for Krishna Consciousness v. Lee*, 505 U.S. 672 (1992).

[25] Ibid., 678–679 (internal citations omitted).

[26] *Capital Sq. Review Bd. v. Pinette*, 515 U.S. 753 (1995).

[27] *Widmar v. Vincent*, 454 U.S. 263 (1981).

[28] Ibid., 269–270.

[29] *Lamb's Chapel v. Ctr. Moriches Sch. Dist.*, 508 U.S. 384 (1993).

[30] *Rosenberger v. Rector of Univ. of Virginia*, 515 U.S. 819 (1995).

[31] *Good News Club v. Milford Cent. Sch.*, 533 U.S. 98 (2001).

[32] Ibid., 111.

[33] Fox News, "Christian Club May Not Meet," Fox News Channel, June 12, 2001, http://www.foxnews.com/printer_friendly_story/(0,3566,27008,00. html, accessed January 17, 2005; "Christian Club May Not Meet Despite Court Ruling," Catholic World News, June 12, 2001, http://www.cwnews/cp,/news/viewstory.cfm?recnum=15719, accessed January 17, 2005.

Chapter Eleven

[1] *Watson v. Jones*, 80 U.S. 679 (1871).

[2] Ibid., 728–729.

[3] *Smith v. Swormstedt*, 57 U.S. 288 (1853).

[4] *Bouldin v. Alexander*, 82 U.S. 131 (1872).

[5] Ibid., 139–140.

[6] *Shepard v. Barkley*, 247 U.S. 1 (1918). The facts are taken from the district court case, *Barkley v. Hayes*, 208 F. 319 (W.D.Mo. 1913). See also *Shepherd v. Barkley*, 222 F. 669 (8th Cir. 1915).

[7] In two earlier cases arising out of the same union, the Supreme Court held that the federal courts had jurisdiction to hear the property disputes. See *Helm v. Zarecor*, 222 U.S. 32 (1911); *Sharpe v. Bonham*, 224 U.S. 241 (1912).

[8] *Gonzalez v. Roman Catholic Archbishop*, 280 U.S. 1 (1929).

[9] *Kedroff v. St. Nicholas Cathedral,* 344 U.S. 94 (1952).

[10] Ibid., 107.

[11] Ibid., 110.

[12] *Kreshik v. St. Nicholas Cathedral,* 363 U.S. 190 (1960).

[13] *Presbyterian Church v. Hull Church,* 393 U.S. 440 (1969).

[14] Ibid., 449.

[15] *Maryland & Virginia Eldership of the Church of God v. Church of God at Sharpsburg, Inc.,* 396 U.S. 367 (1970).

[16] *Serbian Eastern Orthodox Diocese v. Milivojevich,* 426 U.S. 696 (1976).

[17] Ibid., 708.

[18] Ibid., 714–715.

[19] Ibid., 724–725.

[20] *Jones v. Wolf,* 443 U.S. 595 (1979).

[21] Ibid., 603.

[22] *Watson,* n. 1 at 735.

Chapter Twelve

[1] Tocqueville, Alexis de, *Democracy in America,* Vol. I, Reissue Edition, Edited by Phillips Bradley (New York: Vintage Books, 1990), 308.

[2] Ibid.

[3] Ibid., 312.

[4] *Lemon v. Kurtzman,* 403 U.S. 602 (1971).

[5] *Employment Division v. Smith,* 494 U.S. 872 (1990).

[6] *Braunfeld v. Brown,* 366 U.S. 599 (1961); *Frazee v. Illinois Dep't of Employment Security,* 489 U.S. 829 (1989).

[7] *Van Orden v. Perry,* No. 03–1500 (Sup. Ct. Jun. 27, 2005).

[8] *O'Lone v. Estate of Shabazz,* 482 U.S. 342 (1987).

[9] *Cutter v. Wilkinson,* No. 03–9877 (Sup. Ct. May 31, 2005).

[10] *Wooley v. Maynard,* 430 U.S. 705 (1977); *Smith,* n. 5.

[11] *Zobrest v. Catalina Foothills Sch. Dist.,* 509 U.S. 1 (1993); *Zelman v. Simmons-Harris,* 536 U.S. 639 (2002). Chief Justice Rehnquist wrote the majority opinion in *Zobrest* joined by Justices White, Scalia, Kennedy, and Thomas; Justices Blackmun, Souter, Stevens, and O'Connor dissented. Chief Justice Rehnquist also wrote the majority opinion in *Zelman* joined by Justices O'Connor, Scalia, Kennedy, and Thomas; Justices Stevens, Souter, Ginsburg, and Breyer dissented.

[12] *Smith,* n 5; *O'Lone,* n. 8; *Goldman v. Weinberger,* 475 U.S. 503 (1986). In *Smith,* Justice Scalia wrote the majority opinion joined by Chief Justice Rehnquist and Justices White, Stevens, and Kennedy; Justice O'Connor concurred in the judgment; and Justices Blackmun, Brennan, and Marshall dissented. In *O'Lone,* Chief Justice Rehnquist wrote the majority opinion joined by Justices White, Powell, O'Connor, and Scalia, with Justices Brennan, Marshall, Blackmun, and Stevens dissenting. In *Goldberg,* Justice Rehnquist wrote the majority opinion joined by Chief Justice Burger and

Justices White, Powell, and Stevens; Justices Brennan, Marshall, Blackmun, and O'Connor dissented.

[13] *Santa Fe Indep. Sch. Dist. v. Doe*, 530 U.S. 290 (2000); *Lee v. Weisman*, 505 U.S. 577 (1992); *Edwards v. Aguillard*, 482 U.S. 578 (1987). In *Santa Fe*, Justice Stevens wrote the majority opinion joined by Justices O'Connor, Kennedy, Souter, Ginsburg, and Breyer; Chief Justice Rehnquist and Justices Scalia and Thomas dissented. In *Lee*, Justice Kennedy wrote the majority opinion joined by Justices Blackmun, Stevens, O'Connor, and Souter; Chief Justice Rehnquist and Justices Scalia, White, and Thomas dissented. In *Edwards*, Justice Brennan wrote the majority opinion joined by Justices Marshall, Blackmun, Powell, Stevens, and O'Connor (in part). Justice White concurred in the judgment, and Chief Justice Rehnquist and Justice Scalia dissented.

[14] This definition comes from *The American Heritage Dictionary of the English Language*, 4th ed. (Boston: Houghton Mifflin Company, 2000), 1530.

[15] *Everson v. Bd. of Educ.*, 330 U.S. 1, 27 (1947) (Jackson, J., dissenting).

Appendix A

[1] Taken from the *Annals of Congress, Gales & Seaton's History*, House of Representatives, August 15, 1789, copied from images on the Library of Congress web site at http://memory.loc.gov/ammem/amlaw/lawhome.html.

Appendix B

[1] James Madison, "Memorial and Remonstrance Against Religious Assessments," 1785, available on the University of Virginia Library web site at http://religiousfreedom.lib.virginia.edu/sacred/madison_m&r_1785.html (accessed January 20, 2006). An image of the original handwritten document can be viewed on the Library of Congress web site at http://memory.loc.gov/master/mss/mjm/02/0400/0449d.jpg.

SUPREME COURT CASE INDEX

GENERAL INDEX

ABOUT THE AUTHOR

Kathryn Page Camp has been a regulatory attorney for over twenty-five years. As Associate General Counsel for National Futures Association in Chicago, Illinois, she spends much of her time interpreting statutes and case law, writing rules, and drafting proposed legislation. Her professional memberships include the American Bar Association and the Chicago Bar Association.

After receiving her BA from Hope College in 1972, Kathryn went on to earn an MS from DePaul University (1974), a JD from Chicago-Kent College of Law (1978), and an LLM from Chicago-Kent (1999).

Kathryn and her husband, Roland, have two children and live in Northwest Indiana.